OUR THOUGHTS DETERMINE OUR LIVES

THE LIFE AND TEACHINGS OF ELDER THADDEUS OF VITOVNICA

Compiled by the St. Herman of Alaska Brotherhood

Translated by Ana Smiljanic

SAINT HERMAN OF ALASKA BROTHERHOOD

2017

Copyright © 2009, 2017 by the
St. Herman of Alaska Brotherhood
P. O. Box 70
Platina, CA 96076

website: www.sainthermanpress.com
email: stherman@stherman.com

First edition: 2009
Second printing: 2010
Third printing: 2011
Fourth printing: 2012
Fifth printing: 2014
Sixth printing: 2015
Seventh printing: 2017

Printed in the United States of America

Front and back covers: Elder Thaddeus. Photographs by Goran Veljkovic.

Publishers Cataloging in Publication

Our thoughts determine our lives : the life and teachings of Elder Thaddeus of Vitovnica / compiled by the St. Herman of Alaska Brotherhood; translated by Ana Smiljanic.—1st ed.—Platina, CA : St. Herman of Alaska Brotherhood, c2009. 7th printing, c2017.

p. ; cm.

ISBN: 978-1-887904-19-3
Includes bibliographical references and index.

1. Shtrbulovich, Tadej, 1914–2003. 2. Clergy—Serbia—Biography. 3. Spiritual life. 4. Christian life—Orthodox Eastern Church. I. Smiljanic, Ana. II. St. Herman of Alaska Brotherhood. III. Title.

BX395.S58 O87 2009 2009935762   2009935762
281.9/092—dc22   0910

CONTENTS

Elder Thaddeus of Vitovnica.

FOREWORD

Make peace with yourself, and both heaven
and earth will make peace with you.

—St. Isaac the Syrian

Elder Thaddeus of Vitovnica was one of the foremost elders of twentieth-century Serbia. His counsels comforted thousands of people, especially during the dark days of Communism in Serbia, when every attempt was made to mock and undermine the Christian Faith. His words of peace, humility, and love were disseminated in the form of typewritten photocopies, cassette recordings, and through the testimony of his many spiritual children.

For much of his life, Archimandrite Thaddeus (Shtrbulovich) lived in obscurity, laboring for his salvation and praying for the world. Not until the 1970s, when Fr. Thaddeus was over sixty years old, did people begin to flock to him, seeking counsel, healing, and consolation.

Born at the start of the First World War, Elder Thaddeus saw both the establishment of Yugoslavia in 1918 and its tragic collapse at the end of the twentieth century. In between these two monumental events, Fr. Thaddeus endured the privations of war, Nazi imprisonment, and persecution by Tito's Communist government. Despite all of these hardships, Fr. Thaddeus never lost faith in God, always striving to achieve communion with Him through the Sacraments of the Church and the prayer of the heart.

From his childhood, Fr. Thaddeus was occupied with the

meaning of this life and the importance of thoughts. His struggle to understand the purpose of existence led him to see that our lives must be dedicated to serving others, and first of all, God. At the same time, he clearly saw—like his contemporary Elder Paisios of Mount Athos—that our thoughts can create heaven or hell around us in this world. He would return again and again to these themes throughout his life.

Through the influence of the traditions of the Optina and Valaam Monasteries, Fr. Thaddeus learned the art of prayer. At the Miljkovo Monastery in Serbia, where he became a novice in 1932, he became the spiritual son of Schema-archimandrite Ambrose, who was himself a disciple of the Optina Elders. It was through him that Fr. Thaddeus received the gift of Grace-filled prayer—the memory of which would light his way during the darkest years of the twentieth century. At Miljkovo, he was likewise a witness to the deep spiritual tradition of the Russian monks from Valaam, who had been uprooted from their beloved monastery.

Elder Thaddeus, despite his Grace-filled beginnings in the spiritual life, spent many years fighting against the very ailments that afflict so many people in our own era: stress, depression, and nervousness. Because of his own experience in warring against these life-destroying diseases, he was able to console and comfort the thousands of visitors who came to him later in his life. His counsel was always tailored for whoever was in front of him, but at the same time he never strayed far from his central instruction: "Our life depends on the kind of thoughts we nurture. If our thoughts are peaceful, calm, meek, and kind, then that is what our life is like. If our attention is turned to the circumstances in which we live, we are drawn into a whirlpool of thoughts and can have neither peace nor tranquility."

Although few people in the West have heard of Elder Thaddeus, his words and life provide essential insights for our times. He understood the extent to which the philosophy of the modern age has wreaked devastation on the soul of man: through war, environmental destruction and, most importantly, man's turning away from God. Elder Thaddeus saw that the only cure for man's illness was a return to a life centered on Christ the God-man, the only One Who can fulfill all of mankind's needs.

May this book bring relief to all those burdened by the sorrows and uncertainties of our times, that they may turn their gaze to the One Who Is, our eternal Savior and Lord Jesus Christ.

Ryassaphore-monk Adrian
July 18/31, 2009

EDITORS' NOTES:

All footnotes have been supplied by the editors.

This book has been compiled primarily from materials originally published in the Serbian book Peace and Joy in the Holy Spirit. *For more information, see Acknowledgments at the end of the book.*

Map of Serbia, showing monasteries and some of the places
mentioned in the Life of Elder Thaddeus.

PART ONE

THE LIFE OF ELDER THADDEUS

Elder Thaddeus.

THE LIFE OF ELDER THADDEUS

Childhood and Youth

Elder Thaddeus (Shtrbulovich) was born on October 6/19, 1914, on the feast day of the Holy Apostle Thomas, in whose honor he was given the name Tomislav in Holy Baptism. Two months premature, he was born at a village fair into a family of farmers from the village of Vitovnica near the town of Petrovac on the Mlava River. He was baptized immediately after birth, for his parents feared that their prematurely born infant would not live, as he barely showed any signs of life. He only opened his eyes after Baptism. As a child he was weak and sickly. When he became a monastic later in life, he sometimes joked humbly at his own expense, saying, "Well, nothing good could have come out of me anyway, since I was born at a village fair!"

Tomislav had little joy during his childhood while growing up in a poor family during the First World War and the postwar years. His mother died when he was still a young child. Instead of quiet and tender maternal words, the sharp voice of one, then another, stepmother dominated his home. To escape the harshness of everyday life—in which the frail boy with an extremely sensitive soul saw much sorrow—Tomislav resorted to living in his own world of thoughts and reflections. As he later recounted, on more than one occasion he fled from home with only a crust of bread in his pocket. He bore no resemblance to the other children in either stature, constitution, or character. This was his cross: he was different, even in respect to eating. As far back as he could remember, he could not eat anything prepared with lard, and he neither ate eggs nor drank milk. He could not bring himself even to taste meat. For this he was often scolded and forced to eat, but his system would not accept any food of animal origin. Until his sixteenth year he lived mostly on bread, onions, and cucumbers. He was born into this world as into a foreign land—to fast and to live in chastity from his earliest childhood. He grew up a child-ascetic and departed this life for the Kingdom of Heaven as an elder-ascetic.

Frequently chastised and ridiculed, regarded as incapable of work and generally useless in life, Tomislav could look for no solace in this world. "You're not good for anything. Look at Mladen [a neighbor of the same age as Tomislav]. Now that's a lad—helps his father and all! You just sit there and eat your bread for free!" These words hurt little Tomislav so much that he would run to the fields to sit under a tree. There, in the dewy grass, all alone in the world, he would pray for consolation and beseech the Lord to let him be of use too. He was constantly oppressed by the fear that his elders would not be satisfied with him. (This fear also tormented him during the first years of his life as a monastic.)

There is no doubt that the soul of the little boy was also burdened by sadness because his father, a quiet and kind man, failed to protect him and to treat him as he, a child hungry for his father's love, had hoped. "I was disappointed because my father remarried after my mother's death and had two children with his new wife. I was even more disappointed when he married for the third time, because his second wife also died. Poor soul, the only reason he remarried was to have a woman about the house to take care of his children. Because of this war that I waged in my thoughts against my father, I was not able to grow spiritually for a very long time."

God began to reveal to Tomislav at a very early age the mystery of thought and the noetic life: the concentration of thought and the struggle against distractions of the mind. "Even as a child I pondered much upon everything. As a young boy I paid special attention to my thoughts. Now that I am old, I can see that I have yet to reach the degree of understanding of thoughts that I had as a child, for the Lord enlightens children. I was very young and had not yet started school when I noticed that my thoughts wandered while playing with other children. 'This is not good,' I told myself, 'I must be present here in my thoughts, concentrating only on the task I am performing.' But it was to no avail—my thoughts kept wandering."

During those years the boy conceived in his heart a heavenly feeling of not belonging to this world as well as a mystical desire to free himself from a world of sorrow and sadness, to dedicate himself entirely to God, and to seek comfort only in the quiet Lord, Who is the sole Comforter of all who suffer. The Living God softly spoke to the soul that had nowhere to lay its head (cf. Matt. 8:20). "When I understood that neither parents, nor family, nor friends, nor anyone in the world could offer me anything but pain, insults, and wounds, I resolved to stop living for the world and to dedicate my few remaining days in this life to the Lord. I understood that I had no one in the world except God." Simultaneously, God enlightened the boy's mind to the knowledge that our earthly life consists of nothing but serving others, and that, in fact, there is no life other than that of serving and patiently bearing sorrow and pain. "I realized at a very early age that serving is what life is all about. Parents serve their children, and children serve their parents. It was then that a thought came to me: since everyone is here to serve someone else, I want to serve God, because He is above everyone else. See, that's how God calls one from one's earliest days."

Although his childhood and early youth were, through Divine providence, painted in the colors of late autumn rather than spring, Elder Thaddeus always spoke with boundless love about his mother, from whom, as he said, he had inherited a sensitivity of soul, and about his father, who was a "quiet and meek man, unbelievably good-natured." Until his last days, Elder Thaddeus said that he suffered a lot because he had insulted his father in his thoughts, and that he could never repent enough over this. He always instructed his spiritual children on the importance of being obedient, both physically and in one's thoughts, to one's biological parents, for it is they who are, after the Lord, "our greatest good here on this earth." He always taught them that the goal of Christian life was to return to the embrace of our Heavenly Father, the return of the Prodigal Son from the far country to the Land of the Living. "Throughout my whole life I was tormented by thoughts of the goal of our life—I often asked myself where we were going. Was life only about struggling to achieve material wealth, eating and drinking; was that the meaning of life? Thank God, when we read the life of St. Seraphim of Sarov, the saint himself explains to us that the goal of our life is to return to the bosom of our Heavenly Father, in order that we, the men of this earth, may become as the angels, who are guided by the Holy Spirit."

After he finished primary school with excellent marks, his parents sent him to Petrovac to learn the tailor's trade—seeing that because of his poor health and physical weakness he was not fit to work the land. He completed his studies in trade and commerce in Petrovac, but he was unsuccessful in this new job, and suffered much at the hands of cruel and unfeeling people.

The Monastic Call

In 1932, eighteen-year-old Tomislav was completely occupied with thoughts concerning the meaning of life. Out of the depths of his heart arose the desire to become a monk. He wrote a letter to the brotherhood of Gornjak Monastery, begging them to accept him as a novice. God's providence willed that he should wait six months for an answer. What happened in the meantime greatly influenced his future. While waiting for an answer from the

Gornjak Monastery church and gates.

monastery, Tomislav fell gravely ill with pulmonary disease and had to be taken to Belgrade for treatment. He spent forty-seven days in the hospital. Because of his poor health and slight build, his condition did not improve.

"A medical council was formed to decide on my further treatment. After debating for some time, they prescribed a very complicated and painful therapy for me: pneumothorax, a difficult and torturous procedure of injecting oxygen combined with medications into my lungs. I had heard from other patients that this therapy was very painful and exhausting and that even physically stronger patients struggled through it, and so I said to my doctor, 'If you have any other kind of medication for me—fine. If not, I am not willing to undergo this therapy.' The doctors became very angry. 'Who are you to teach us how to cure people!' they said. 'You are to come tomorrow to the tuberculosis department to start with your therapy!'

"'Well,' I thought, 'it's highly unlikely that you will see me there tomorrow.' I asked them how long I would live without this therapy of theirs. One woman doctor told me, 'If you agree to take this therapy you may be cured of your illness, but if not, you certainly will not live longer than five years.' And I thought, 'So they are not even sure of the outcome of the therapy!' I accepted my condition and decided to spend the remaining five years of my life serving God. However, a new problem arose: my parents did not agree with my decision.

"But my commitment would not allow me to be at peace [with my parents' objections], and so I went to the Gornjak Monastery against my parents' will. I arrived there in the late evening hours, just as the abbot [Fr. Seraphim] was coming out of the church after Vespers. He received me kindly. I told him about my decision to dedicate my life to the service of God and explained to him my understanding of the monastic life. A Russian monk sat with us. I cannot remember exactly what I said to the abbot. Before Liturgy the following day, I caught a glimpse of the Russian monk taking the *prosphora*,[1] wine, and water to church. He went into the church and I followed him. He took the prosphora, wine, and water into the altar, and I venerated the icons. When he came out of the altar, he said to me, 'I heard what you were talking about with the abbot. I heard your thoughts on monasticism. You are not going to find the kind of monasticism you are looking for anywhere in Serbia except among the Russian monks of the Miljkovo Monastery. The brotherhood of that monastery is made up of monks exiled from Valaam Monastery in Finland.'

"'This is where you should go,' the monk told me. 'It is only there that you can find what your soul desires.' I was uncertain as to whether they would accept me and said so. 'They will,' answered the monk."

This took place on July 24/August 6, 1932.

Miljkovo Monastery: In the Paradise of First Grace

Miljkovo Monastery was at that time home to Russian monastics, many of whom had come to Serbia from the well-known monastery of Valaam, persecuted by their own kin. In 1918 the Valaam Islands, the "Mount Athos of the North," were annexed from Russia and became a part of Finland. Valaam Monastery thus fell under the jurisdiction of the Finnish Orthodox Church, which would accept the New Calendar in 1921. After a great struggle, in 1925 the Finnish Church authorities forced Valaam Monastery to accept the New Calendar. Most of the monks faithful to the Church Calendar of the Russian Orthodox Church were banished from the monastery between 1925 and 1927. By Divine providence many of them came to Serbia, were accepted by the Church, and given a place in Serbian monasteries. A number of the monks came to Miljkovo Monastery.

Their spiritual father was Schema-archimandrite Ambrose

[1] *Prosphora:* small loaves of bread prepared for the Divine Liturgy.

Archpriest Peter Perekrestov Archive

The Miljkovo Monastery brotherhood during Fr. Ambrose's abbacy. At center is Metropolitan Anthony (Khrapovitsky); next to him (on left) is Schema-archimandrite Ambrose.

(Kurganov) (†1933),[1] a spiritual child of the Optina Elders.[2] These monks brought with them the hesychastic spirit of coenobitic monasticism that Valaam had shared in common with Optina. The Miljkovo Monastery adhered to the strict Valaam typicon[3]

[1] See Archbishop Antony (Medvedev) of San Francisco, *The Young Elder: A Biography of Blessed Archimandrite Ambrose of Milkovo* (Jordanville, N.Y.: Holy Trinity Russian Orthodox Monastery, 1974).

[2] The Optina Hermitage was a center for spiritual revival and eldership in nineteenth-century Russia. Optina's spiritual foundations were the teachings of St. Paisius (Velichkovsky) (1722–1794), who rediscovered on Mount Athos the writings of the Holy Fathers on noetic prayer. The first Optina Elders were Sts. Leo, Macarius, Moses, and Anthony.

[3] *Typicon:* the order of Divine services. Also, the rules and ordinances of a particular monastery.

and the services were typically "Russian," often lasting for many hours. The monks obeyed a rigorous fasting rule, and the cell prayer rules were long and tiring. The Holy Liturgy was served daily. Throughout his entire life as a hieromonk,[1] Fr. Thaddeus strove to fulfill the Valaam prayer rule and to serve the Holy Liturgy every day, even when he was very ill. He often repeated the words of St. John of Kronstadt: "When I am not serving the Holy Liturgy, I feel as though I am dying!"

Many years later Fr. Thaddeus would recount his arrival at the monastery: "At the gate of the Miljkovo Monastery, I saw a young novice and asked him if the abbot was there. He was. The young novice agreed to take me to him. The abbot had rolled up his robe and was treading mud mixed with chaff with his bare feet. He looked at me and said, 'So, you want to be a monk, do you?' I said I did. 'Good,' he said. 'I'm building a *banya*[2] for the brethren.'

"He instructed the novice to take me to the refectory and to give me some food. 'Give him a cell, too, so that he can rest. There will be a vigil tonight. This young man is not used to our long vigils.' The vigil was indeed very long. It began at six and ended at eleven o'clock. They served the Holy Liturgy and the full cycle of prayers every day. After a week had gone by, the abbot called me to him and asked me, 'Do you like it here? Would you like to stay?' I answered that I very much wanted to stay. 'Good,' said the abbot. 'I have already talked to Fr. Paul.' Fr. Paul was from Bosnia, an elderly monk about seventy years old. He had lived in America for many years, and when he returned to Serbia he originally became a monk at the Gornjak Monastery. 'Fr. Paul takes care of the vineyards. Near the vineyard there is a small house. That is where he sleeps. You will take care of the vineyard now, and Fr. Paul will come down to the monastery to help the brethren. He is an experienced monk.' And so I stayed at the Miljkovo Monastery."

[1] *Hieromonk:* a monk who has been ordained to the priesthood.
[2] *Banya:* a Russian sauna or sweat-house.

Archpriest Peter Perekrestov Archive

Schema-archimandrite Ambrose.

There were about thirty monks in the monastery. Schema-archimandrite Ambrose was the living sun of the Miljkovo Monastery and an ascetic who lived a holy life. As a novice he had been under the guidance of Elder Theodosius, the superior of the Optina Skete.[1] Fr. Ambrose had the gift of unceasing prayer and lived in constant remembrance of death. He emanated the joy and peacefulness of the Kingdom of God. Fr. Thaddeus, who until the end of his earthly life nurtured a burning love for his spiritual

---

[1] Elder Theodosius (1854–1920) was both the disciple and confessor of Elder Barsanuphius of Optina. He was the Skete superior from 1912 until 1920.

teacher, said of him, "Fr. Ambrose radiated an unbelievable and pure love. He had received the best gift of all from the Optina Elders—love. He never became angry with any of his monks or novices and never uttered a sharp word to them. He bore everything with patience and forgave everyone. He placed all of his cares and burdens at the feet of the Lord and confided all his sorrows only to Him. He strove to pass all of this on to the brotherhood of his monastery, and many of them learned how to nurture and apply this all-encompassing and passionless love in their everyday lives."

It was with this spirit of Divine love that Elder Ambrose, himself an example of righteous living, kindled a spark in the pure soul of Br. Tomislav, for whom this Divine love would always remain as the only measure of true life. Fr. Ambrose "would always be the first to arrive in church for the services and stand beside the abbot's chair. One could see that he was heavily burdened with cares for the monastery, but he never complained to anyone, confiding only in God. He never punished anyone or held a bad thought about anyone, let alone looked at anyone with anger. He loved everyone just as they were and prayed to God to enlighten them. He taught others mostly by his own example, through which he strove to lead everyone onto the path of salvation."

The first days at the monastery were ones of the greatest joy for Br. Tomislav. Immersing himself in the mystical relationship between spiritual father and son, he learned from Fr. Ambrose about holy and salvific obedience, vigilance over his thoughts, and the Jesus Prayer.[1] "Fr. Ambrose said to me, 'Whatever you do, always silently repeat these words: Lord Jesus Christ, Son of God, have mercy on me, a sinner!' I was a young lad and I obeyed him with all my heart. Each night I would confess before my spiritual father and tell him what was happening within my soul, and he

---

[1] *Jesus Prayer:* A short prayer directed to Jesus Christ, using the words "Lord Jesus Christ, Son of God, have mercy on me, a sinner"—or variants thereof.

would counsel me." The novice, believing that he had only five years left to live, gave himself completely over to the prayer of the heart. "In a very short while, because of my complete surrender to the will of God and sincere longing for Him, I was enlightened by the Grace of God, which created an indescribable feeling of joy and peace. I listened to my heart and inside it I heard the words 'Lord Jesus Christ, Son of God, have mercy on me, a sinner.' I tried to remember certain events from the past and I could not; all my thoughts were at peace and a feeling of ineffable joy and longing reigned in my entire being. Such is the state of the angels and the saints, a state of complete and perfect Grace. Only those who have experienced the gift of Grace understand the state of the angels and the saints, who are led by the Holy Spirit." Thus Tomislav became the humble receptacle of the hesychastic spirit of the Church, adorned by the fragrant blossom of the prayer of the heart.

Later, Fr. Thaddeus would repeatedly tell his spiritual children about "gratuitous Grace" as a priceless gift from God, through which God guides us in our spiritual life, in the beginning showing us the goal of our life—deification in Christ within the Church—and in times of sorrow and suffering giving us strength and comfort. Being inexperienced in the spiritual life, Br. Tomislav thought that all monks possess this God-bestowed gratuitous Grace, and it was only much later that he understood that God's love had made him worthy of a great and undeserved gift, preparing him for the Golgotha of his future service as an abbot and a spiritual father to many. "I thought that all monastics, priests and bishops had the gift of gratuitous Grace and—would you believe it?—I have spent so many years now among monks and priests, and I have met only one monk who had this gift. Only one! However, among lay people who live with their families, I have encountered many individuals who have received this gift of Grace."

Br. Tomislav's health gradually improved due to the strict

Miljkovo Monastery Church of the Entry of the Theotokos into the Temple. Photo taken during the time of Schema-archimandrite Ambrose.

fasting in the monastery. Still, he was physically weak, and he would often fall asleep while going about his obediences.[1] "When I first came to Miljkovo, I was given the obedience of working in the vineyards. As I was not very good at staying awake, I fell asleep as I was guarding the vineyards, and robbers came and stole the grapes. I waited in fear for the steward of the monastery to come to the vineyard. The steward came and saw what had happened, yet he did not say a word to me! The grapes were stolen, yet he did not reproach me. He came to me the following day and said, 'Tomushka' (that was how they called me at the monastery while I was still a novice), '*Batiushka*[2] has blessed me to give you a new obedience. You will guard the sheep and goats on the fields close to the Morava River.' And so I became a shepherd. However, I made a mistake again very soon after that.

"They had given me the *Horologion*[3] in order that I might practice reading from it, and while I was reading the book, I fell asleep again. When I woke up, I looked for the sheep, but all I could see was one old goat. I sprang up to look for them. What did I see? They had made a hole in one of the fences and had wandered off to some farmer's field, and were happily chewing away on his crop. The goat saw me running toward the sheep and followed me, almost bringing down the entire fence. The owner of the field saw what had happened and went straight to the abbot of the monastery to complain. The abbot told the steward to pay the farmer to cover his loss and that was the end of it. Not one of the brothers said a word about the whole thing, not a word! The steward came to me again in the morning and said, 'Batiushka has blessed me to give you a new obedience. From now on you will be taking care of the cows on the other side of the field.'

[1] *Obedience:* in addition to its ordinary meaning, it signifies some duty assigned and carried out as part of one's obedience to the superior or elder.

[2] *Batiushka:* an endearing term for a priest or monk.

[3] *Horologion:* The Book of Hours, which contains the fixed portions of the daily services.

"A similar thing happened. We had six cows. Among them was an old cow who seemed to like doing damage. I kept counting the cows so as not to make the same mistake again. I also brought my Horologion with me and read it from time to time. As I was reading, the old cow managed to steal away and go to the fields on the other side. I sat there reading my Horologion, looking at the cows from time to time. It appeared to me that all six of them were there. However, when I counted them carefully, I saw that the old cow was not there. I became numb with fear and ran to look for it. When I looked in the cabbage patches, the runaway cow was already eating away the third cabbage patch, having previously trampled all over it. Again the farmer complained to the abbot and again the steward gave me a new obedience. My new duty was to be in the refectory and in the church.

"These are only a few of my trials which Elder Ambrose covered with his immeasurable love. Later there were worse and more painful ones, but the elder responded to each of them only with his love. There was a monk who had previously held an important position in the Russian government. He liked to drink wine a lot. He would even leave the monastery and disappear for a week. The abbot had to look for him in the village, where he spent his time doing nothing but drinking. One would think that the abbot would chastise him for his behavior, but no—not a word from Elder Ambrose. He loved him all the same, as though nothing had happened."

From that time on, Novice Tomislav began his tripartite, lifelong endeavor: that of repentant striving for Christ's Grace, which is the only true life for man; that of vigilance in the state of Grace when it was given to him by God; and that of tears and repentant sorrow whenever this gift was taken away from him. "I was very interested in learning how the Holy Fathers felt during their earthly lives and how they were able to preserve the state of gratuitous Grace to the very end," he once said. He understood that Grace could only be preserved by constant vigilance over

St. John (Maximovitch) of Shanghai and San Francisco (then Hieromonk
John) with students at the Bitola Seminary, 1931.

the heart and mind and by prayer: "If you wish to preserve this
gift of Grace, you must pray to God all the time in order to block
oppressive and dark thoughts from your mind and thus preserve
the peace and joy which you feel when you are illumined by
Grace."

God also made Br. Tomislav worthy of an encounter with
Hieromonk John (Maximovitch), who later became Bishop of
Shanghai and then of San Francisco, and after his repose was
canonized. Fr. Thaddeus would later recall: "He was a teacher
at the Seminary in Bitola, and during the summer holidays he
would often come to Miljkovo monastery to spend the summer.
The steward at the monastery at that time was Fr. Peter, who had
once been governor of a very large region in imperial Russia, larger
even than Serbia. He told all of us to go and weed the monastery
gardens. I was to work with Hieromonk John.... He was weeding
the vegetable garden from one side, and I was weeding from the
other. I asked him a few questions and he told me about the lives
of the saints and we spent quite some time in conversation.

"Now, Fr. Peter noticed this and began to chastise Fr. John. 'What do you think, entertaining this young novice here, when there's work to be done!' And Fr. John answered, 'Forgive me, Batiuska, forgive me. I'll do my job!' He was very pious and had had many spiritual experiences. He read the Holy Fathers a lot and knew many soul-edifying things, so when he would start talking, I would stop everything I was doing and listen."

The battle with thoughts—which Br. Tomislav had experienced and whose mystical depths he had touched even as a young child—began in earnest when he became a monk. He began to understand, based on his own experience, that being a Christian meant waging a constant and merciless battle against evil and death in one's own heart, a battle with no front lines or cease-fires, in which the enemy neither sleeps nor tires. "Like any monk, I struggled and prayed to God, I made many prostrations and said many prayers. I always lived in fear lest the devil appear to me in the form of an angel or a saint, but the Lord once actually permitted the devil to appear to me. Once, when I was standing before the holy icons, he stood in front of me so that I would bow down before him. I crossed myself and called upon the name of the Lord, but he said, 'I am not afraid of the Cross!' I began to say my prayers, but he said, 'I am not afraid of prayers, either!' And so he tormented me. I went to my elder, and he told me that I was probably not praying fervently enough. I told him that I prayed from the heart, but that the demon tormented me night and day, grinning at me. What was I to do? O Lord, I had no idea how to rid myself of him; I had no peace or rest. Then my elder told me that repentance was very important, and that I was to pray with contrition, from the heart, and he would go away."

Besides learning to perform various monastery obediences, Br. Tomislav also mastered the Russian language. This enabled him to read zealously the works of the Holy Fathers which were translated into Russian from the Greek and Syrian languages.

Archpriest Peter Perekrestov Archive

Schema-archimandrite Ambrose (on left) at the Miljkovo Monastery.

He also undertook to translate some of these texts into Serbian, including *The Homilies of St. Isaac the Syrian*. This would one day prove to be of great significance for him, when he found himself in the same situation as St. Paisius (Velichkovsky): in the eighteenth century St. Paisius was unable to obtain a spiritual father, but he found spiritual guidance in the God-enlightened mind and experience of the Holy Fathers, expressed in their theology and teachings.

As it so often happens in life, this state of heavenly joy would not last long, for God—as Fr. Thaddeus explained—does not permit an inexperienced person to enjoy the state of Grace for very long, in order that he might not abuse it. Elder Ambrose fell asleep in the Lord in 1933, only one year after Tomislav arrived at the monastery. He experienced great sorrow; he lost the prayer of the heart, and God's Grace departed from him. "When my spiritual father died, I spent many years in sorrow and pain. My soul was torn asunder by sadness. The fears that had tormented me in childhood came back."

In an attempt to heal his soul, he would take up his accordion and go into the hills where he would spend hours in solitude playing music. "I had always loved music and this brought me comfort." He also sought consolation from other elders, but his soul could not be comforted. Just when all hope abandoned him, God sent him consolation through a copy of *The Path to Salvation* by St. Theophan the Recluse. Thus, the experience of the Holy Fathers was confirmed once more in the life of Tomislav. "When there is no human being that can bring us comfort, then God comes and brings us joy through a book."

Tonsure and Ordination

After the repose of Elder Ambrose of Miljkovo, there arose a conflict as to who would be his successor, and there was much unrest because of this at the monastery. The brotherhood, once united in thought and prayer, now went their separate ways, some to the monastery of Tumane and others to Kalenich. After some time, Novice Tomislav left for the Gornjak Monastery, where, on February 26/March 11, 1935, he received the monastic tonsure from Abbot Seraphim with the name of Thaddeus. On May 19/June 1 of the same year he was ordained a *hierodeacon*.[1]

Soon afterwards he received the blessing from Bishop Benjamin of Branichevo to enter the service of the Archdiocese of Belgrade and Karlovci at the Rakovica Monastery in Belgrade. There, with the blessing of Patriarch Barnabas (Rosich), Fr. Thaddeus finished the school of iconography and became deeply immersed in the study of the mystical theology of the icon. After completing his studies he abandoned painting icons for health reasons. His ailing lungs could not tolerate the evaporation of paint and solvents in a closed room.

Fr. Thaddeus spent the whole of 1937, the year that the

---

[1] *Hierodeacon*: a monk who has been ordained a deacon.

Vladimir Markovic

Contemporary picture of Rakovica Monastery,
where Elder Thaddeus lived in 1935 and 1936.

doctors had said would be his last, under the dark clouds of
the *Concordate*[1] crisis and the mysterious death of Patriarch
Barnabas.[2] He was ordained a hieromonk on January 21/
February 3, 1938, at Rakovica. That same year, while still the
youngest hieromonk of the monastery, he was sent by Patriarch

[1] *Concordate:* leglislation introduced in the Yugoslav parliament in 1937
granting greater privileges to the Roman Catholic Church. It was eventually defeated because of opposition from the Synod of the Serbian Orthodox
Church.

[2] Patriarch Barnabas (Rosich) (1880–1937) was Patriarch of Serbia between 1930 and 1937. This was a time of tremendous growth for the Orthodox Church in the region: new dioceses, churches, and monasteries were
established during this period. He was one of the most vocal opponents of
the Concordate, maintaining that it would undermine the position of the
Serbian Orthodox Church and the other established faiths in Yugoslavia. He
died unexpectedly on the night between July 23 and 24, 1937, when the Concordate legislation was introduced into parliament.

Gabriel (Dozich)[1] to the Patriarchate of Pech in Kosovo and Metohija.

In Pech, Hieromonk Thaddeus encountered unexpected difficulties. Hieromonk John (Zecevich), who was abbot of that monastery from 1939 to 1941, was a Communist Party sympathizer. One of the leading Communists in Pech, a certain Drago Kaludjerovich, often came to the monastery and threatened Fr. Thaddeus and other "reactionary" monks, saying that once the Communists came into power there would be no place for them at the Patriarchate of Pech. Fr. Thaddeus remained there until the outbreak of World War II in Serbia in 1941, when he and the four remaining monks had to flee Pech due to the violence of Albanian terrorists. He returned to Belgrade as a refugee and was once again accepted into the brotherhood of the Rakovica Monastery.

Two Arrests and the Miraculous Appearance of an Angel of God

The residents of Belgrade suffered greatly during the first weeks after the Germans occupied the city, and so Hieromonk Thaddeus attempted to move to the Diocese of Banat under the *omophorion*[2] of Bishop Damascene, who would later become the metropolitan of Zagreb. In Banat there was "plenty of bread, and more than bread, whereas Belgrade had almost no food at all." He was arrested, however, at the railway station in Belgrade because, as a member of the clergy, he seemed suspicious to some German officials. The Nazi occupation forces viewed the Serbian Church as the strongest pillar of Serbian spirit and history, and as such, the Church had to be destroyed if the Serbian people were to be conquered. Fr. Thaddeus was taken to the German Special Police station on the grounds that he was traveling to

---

[1] Patriarch Gabriel (Dozich) (1881–1950) served as the head of the Serbian Orthodox Church from 1937 until 1950.

[2] *Omophorion:* the outer stole worn by Orthodox bishops.

Banat with the aim of organizing insurgent Communist groups. The Germans cross-examined him and finally released him due to lack of evidence.

Once he was out of custody, he went to the monastery of Vitovnica in his native village. However, the murderer and father of lies (cf. John 8:44) did not leave him in peace. Only a few days after arriving in Vitovnica he was summoned to the office of the SS commander of the region, who demanded that Fr. Thaddeus, as a member of the clergy, put himself at the disposal of the occupying forces. He refused politely but firmly, saying that as a priest of the Serbian Orthodox Church he could do nothing without the blessing of his bishop. "Those were hard times," recalled Fr. Thaddeus many years later. "The shadow of death loomed over you if you only so much as said the wrong word or refused to obey a command." However, even under the threat of death, the elder demonstrated a complete submission to the will of God and an exclusive service to Christ and His Body, the Church, which characterized him to the end of his life.

In 1943 the Germans arrested him again, with no known charges, this time in the town of Petrovac. He was thrown into a prison cell with two tobacco smugglers. The German authorities sentenced him to death since he was already in their files due to his previous arrest in Belgrade.

As he lay on the narrow prison bunk, Fr. Thaddeus was convinced that he would never taste freedom again. "I thought that I was never going to get out of there alive. 'The end of my life has come,' I thought, 'my God, my God!'" And as these dark thoughts assailed him, God suddenly raised him up from despair with a wonderful vision. "There I was, desperate as could be, lying on the bench and thinking, 'There is no way out of here.' All of a sudden a tall soldier appeared out of nowhere. He had wide golden bands on his chest tied in the form of a cross. He had something over his forehead; it wasn't a helmet, but it had a beautiful plume over it. His uniform was like something from a

34

fresco. He was a handsome man, tall. I had never seen anything like him in my whole life! He had a scroll in his hand, and he was looking at me. And I knew—it was as clear as day—this was an angel which God had sent to comfort me! He unrolled the scroll of paper and showed it to me. A map of Serbia was drawn on it. He said to me, 'Look! Do not be afraid, do not be frightened, for there are still many of those whom you must comfort and give courage to. Do you understand?' I looked around to see whether my cell-mates had heard any of this conversation. I did not know then that one could communicate with spiritual beings in one's thoughts. Their thoughts echo in one's mind. I turned back to face him but he had disappeared. It was then that I realized that I had beheld a heavenly vision which God had made me worthy of seeing in order to comfort me and make known to me His will regarding my life in this world. The year was 1943, and it was the first and only time I ever saw a messenger of God while awake. Later, I only had revelations in my dreams."

God spoke to Fr. Thaddeus through His angel in one of the most difficult moments of his life, as he was face-to-face with death. In this way he was shown the path he was to walk, the obedience he was to fulfill, and the cross he was to carry: to comfort and give strength to the people of God with Christ's Gospel until his last breath.

In his Via Dolorosa through the Nazi prisons, Hieromonk Thaddeus suffered as a confessor in the collective martyrdom of the clergy and monastics of the Serbian Church. On March 5, 1943, after serving time in the prisons in Petrovac and Pozarevac, he was imprisoned in Vojlovica Monastery. There he met St. Nikolai (Velimirovich), Bishop of Ochrid and Zhicha. According to Hieromonk Basil (Kostich), who had also been imprisoned at Vojlovica, Fr. Thaddeus came to this monastery completely exhausted and lice ridden, but once he had recovered, he served the Holy Liturgy with St. Nikolai and other priests on March 13, 1943.

The church of the
Patriarchate of Pech.

The Postwar Years

After the end of World War II, Hieromonk Thaddeus was to have
returned to the Patriarchate of Pech. Instead, he received a blessing
from Metropolitan Joseph of Skoplje, who was acting as deputy
for the still-imprisoned Patriarch Gabriel,[1] for a transfer to the
Gornjak Monastery in the Branichevo Diocese, in order that he
might find "peace and spiritual joy" there.

In 1949 he was again transferred to the Archdiocese of
Belgrade and Karlovci and was raised to the rank of abbot in
the Cathedral Church in Belgrade by Bishop Visarion. By the
end of the year, however, Patriarch Gabriel sent him again to the

---

[1] Patriarch Gabriel was arrested by the Germans in 1941 for his refusal to
cooperate with the occupying forces. He was later taken with St. Nikolai (Velimirovich) to the death camp at Dachau. At the end of 1946, he was finally
able to return to Belgrade.

Patriarchate of Pech, this time as abbot. Upon his arrival there, he found the monastery in a terrible state: the buildings were neglected and partially destroyed, and several families were living there as refugees. The monastery also served as a Communist headquarters for the local partisans.

"The Communists gave me a lot of trouble. They tried as hard as they could to make life as miserable as possible for me. But, thank God, I survived." While at the Patriarchate of Pech, after a series of temptations and misfortunes which assailed him from both within and without, Fr. Thaddeus began smoking again. (He had smoked before, also at the Patriarchate of Pech.) The nicotine had a terrible effect on him because of his frail nerves. However, after a bitter battle, he managed to free himself of this vice.

As he related many years later to one of his spiritual children, at the time of this inner battle he suffered two nervous breakdowns as a result of the warfare against the temptations of fear, anxiety, and worry. His whole body trembled and he was, overall, in a very bad state. He took this as a warning from God and resolved to change his way of life and drop all earthly cares and worries. "I realized that we all worry about ourselves too much and that only he who leaves everything to the will of God can feel truly joyous, light, and peaceful." Thus, having learned to leave all of his cares and those of his neighbors in the hands of the Lord, he patiently bore the cross of serving as abbot at the Patriarchate of Pech for the next six years.

With the blessing of Bishop Vincent, he returned to the Diocese of Branichevo in 1955, where he was assigned the parishes of Pechane and Klenovo. In 1956 he was again assigned to serve as abbot at the Patriarchate of Pech. He remained there for a year and in 1957, after a total of eleven years at the Patriarchate of Pech (three as a brother and eight as abbot), he again returned to the Metropolitanate of Belgrade and Karlovci. In that same year he became abbot of the Gornjak Monastery, serving the parishes of Sigak and Bliznak, which encompassed three villages.

Hilandar Monastery, Mount Athos.

He remained a humble cleric of the Branichevo Diocese until his repose in 2003.

Like all Christ-loving Serbian monks, Fr. Thaddeus had for many years nurtured a burning desire to make his permanent abode in St. Sava's endowment on the Holy Mountain—the Hilandar Monastery—and there seek the salvation of his soul and the peace necessary for a life of prayer and repentance. It was with this burning desire in mind that he begged his bishop's blessing to visit the Holy Mountain in the mid-fifties. He finally received a blessing from his bishop in 1959, and left for the Holy Mountain shortly thereafter.

However, Hieromonk Thaddeus was not made to feel very welcome at Hilandar. A possible reason for this was that he went there as a fully formed monk, and like many monasteries, the Hilandar Brotherhood preferred beginners and novices to already tonsured monks, who were unused to the Athonite way of life. Also, Fr. Thaddeus had already been an abbot in several coenobitic monasteries. At that time Hilandar was not a coenobitic monastery, neither were there any plans for it to become one.

During his two-month stay at Hilandar, Fr. Thaddeus was granted a miraculous visitation by the Most Holy *Theotokos*.[1] "I did not feel well in Hilandar. I thought I was having heart problems. One night I had a dream: We Athonites were going to get a blessing from the Most Holy Mother of God, the Abbess of Hilandar. The brethren all came up to her one by one to kiss her hand. As I came up to her, I asked her to pray to her Son, our God, to forgive all the sins I had committed in my life. Then I waited for her to speak. 'It is nothing,' she said. 'Your nerves are very worn out.'"

After two months at Hilandar, the brotherhood informed Hieromonk Thaddeus that he had to leave Mount Athos because his visa had expired. Although he had most ardently desired to remain in Hilandar, it was not to be. He later said that all this had happened because his visit to Hilandar had been a product of his own will and not the will of God which had been clearly revealed to him during the angelic visitation in the Petrovac prison in 1943: "There are many in the world whom you must comfort and encourage!" This was something, as he himself said, he often forgot.

Thus God guided him back to Serbia to fulfill his obedience as a guide to salvation for the heavy-laden and needy souls of his fellow men. Upon his return from Hilandar, he served in the Bistrik parish, and later as abbot of the Tumane Monastery. In 1962 he asked to be moved from Tumane to Vitovnica. He became abbot of Vitovnica and served the parish of Vlashki Dol for ten years.

Once, when he was under much pressure from an onslaught of thoughts, he rushed to the monastery, where he gave his confession before one of the younger hieromonks. After this, he was made

---

[1] *Theotokos:* the Greek word for the Mother of God; literally, "God-birthgiver."

worthy of another heavenly vision: Upon waking up in his cell with a feeling of complete inner peace and spiritual renewal, in his mind he heard a heavenly voice saying, "This is how you must ease all tension. Do not take upon yourself the worries of this world too much, but guard your peace and live with God!" God also granted him a miraculous vision on another occasion when, after an exhausting spiritual battle, he found himself in a very bad state. Of this, Fr. Thaddeus says: "The Savior spoke to me and told me to fall down before His Most Holy Mother, the Protectress of monastics."

As a monastic who had longed for a life of silence and reflection from his youth, Fr. Thaddeus never desired the position of abbot. Of this he said: "The duty of abbot was always very hard for me because I had to concentrate on material things and the relationships among the brotherhood and the people.... This is where I kept losing the gift of Grace that I had been given as a novice. This generated all kinds of new difficulties in my spiritual life and damaged my physical health." For a while, Fr. Thaddeus took the advice of doctors and went on medication, which did not help him at all because the elder's illness came as a result of his spiritual warfare, for he was not wrestling *against flesh and blood, but against principalities, against powers, against the rulers of the darkness of this world, against spiritual wickedness in high places* (Eph. 6:12).

There were many instances during his service at the monastery when he begged to be released from his obedience as abbot, not only because he was unable to endure the severe trials of this duty, but because his whole being longed after a life of silence, vigilance, and pure prayer. However, by God's will he was always sent back to his flock and his duties as abbot.

This wrestling with God lasted for many years. "If we ourselves do not learn humility, God will not stop humbling us," were words that Fr. Thaddeus often repeated during the last years of his earthly life when he recounted how he had tried to avoid his obediences and the cross that he had been given by the Lord. Or, as the old Byzantine saying goes: If it is the king that is persecuting you, run; if it is God Who is persecuting you, sit down! And persecute him He did, gently guiding the Christ-loving monk across the map of Serbia revealed to him in the angelic vision in 1943, in order to bring him to perfection and extreme humility in serving all people.

In 1972 Fr. Thaddeus was first sent into retirement and then installed as abbot of the Pokajnica Monastery. In these spiritually difficult years, Fr. Thaddeus was again made worthy of a miraculous vision, a gentle warning from God. "When they sent me to Pokajnica to serve as abbot, I was afraid of the problems that the local people posed. It was then that the Lord Himself came to me in a dream and warned me. Suddenly I found myself face to face with Him. He was wearing an *epitrachelion*,[1] an omophorion over His shoulders, and another epitrachelion over it. I stood gazing at Him as He said, 'Why do you fight the good fight when you have no obedience? Whenever you were assigned to serve at a certain place as abbot you complained about it, asking to be excused. You must not do so anymore! Know that you must carry out every obedience with much love, earnestly, and with zeal, without paying any attention to the envy and malice around you.' Then He made the sign of the Cross over me three times, took off His epitrachelion, and put it over my head, saying, 'This is the cross that you must bear.'" This cross was the cross of blessed eldership and the spiritual guidance of many hungry and thirsty souls.

Consoling through the Words of the Holy Fathers

"Until the year 1975, I was very withdrawn. I never went anywhere; the company of men did not appeal to me in the least—partly

---

[1] *Epitrachelion:* a liturgical stole that hangs from the neck of the priest and is required to be worn for all priestly duties.

Fr. Ron Roberson

Fr. Ron Roberson

Pokajnica Monastery.

because of my health, partly because of my nature," said Fr. Thaddeus. However, at the repeated pleas of Br. Dragi, a devoted missionary, with the blessing of his bishop and driven by love for the Church and her faithful, Fr. Thaddeus began attending spiritual talks and lectures in Krnjevo. "That is where I first met Bishop Athanasius [Yevtich], who was at that time a hieromonk and a professor at the School of Theology. My head was full of the sayings of the Holy Fathers. People would ask me one thing, then another, and I would answer them. They seemed to like what they heard from me. I met many pious lay people who found the answers to all their burning questions in the sayings of the Holy Fathers. Since then people began to come to me more and more often. Now they come to me all the time."

Obeying the voice of the Church, Fr. Thaddeus began a new ascetic labor of tireless and self-crucifying service as a spiritual father to many, which was to last until he departed this life. "I had to talk a lot, and because of this my throat began to give out. It became chronically inflamed, and it is not completely healthy after all these years. There are times when I barely have enough strength in my voice to serve the Holy Liturgy."

In 1978 Fr. Thaddeus told G., one of his spiritual daughters, of another vision he had seen in a dream. "I had barely fallen asleep when I dreamt that I had died. Two young men led me into a room and had me stand on some sort of platform between them. To my right were the judges. Someone in the far left corner of the room was reading the charges against me. 'That's him! That's the one who cannot get along with anyone!' I stood there dumbfounded. The voice repeated the same accusation two more times. Then the young man standing on my right said to me, 'Do not be afraid! It is not true that you cannot get along with anyone. You just cannot get along with yourself!'"

At that moment the words of St. Isaac the Syrian that Fr. Thaddeus had repeated countless times to himself and to his spiritual children became his sole path to salvation: "Make peace

The Vitovnica Church of the Dormition of the Most Holy Theotokos. To the right of the church is the arbor under which Fr. Thaddeus received pilgrims.

with yourself, and both heaven and earth will make peace with you."

When We Pray for Someone,
We Take upon Ourselves His Suffering

After serving as superior of the Pokajnica Monastery, Fr. Thaddeus was again sent to Tumane as abbot, and in 1981 he returned to Vitovnica. Beginning in the early eighties, first rivulets, then streams, and finally rivers of pilgrims and penitents who longed for healing and comfort from God flowed to Fr. Thaddeus from all parts of Serbia, but especially from Belgrade. They came in buses, walked, or drove. A spring of clean water attracts the unclean and the thirsty, who hasten to bathe themselves in it and drink from it. Talks, lessons, spiritual advice, and prayers—all this lasted for hours, far into the night and often into the early hours of morning. Confessions flowed into Liturgy, and vigils into late-night discourses.

Elder Thaddeus welcomed each pilgrim with the same infinite love and attentiveness. He received pilgrims in the small monastery kitchen when the weather was cold, or in the church yard in front of the entrance to the Church of the Dormition of the Most Holy Theotokos, in the shade of the grapevine. "They come to tell me their woes. Sometimes we exchange ideas. Many feel better afterwards. As for me, I talk and talk. Every day. Even if my lungs were made out of steel, I'm sure they would collapse. All this pain and sorrow takes its toll on you. They ask me all sorts of things, but I don't know how to answer; I'm not one for communicating with people. I didn't feel old age creeping up on me until last year. Now I've lost my strength; I can't talk for long. Now the endless rivers of people..., that's the way it has to be, I suppose. However, in the past two months I have been in a lot of spiritual anguish. I have never experienced so much anguish before, not even in the war. I suppose I must taste of this as well."

One pilgrim, in her reminiscences of a visit to Fr. Thaddeus, has written a vivid description of her arrival at the monastery and her meeting with the elder:

As we near the monastery, we pause briefly before the gates. We listen to the silence and take in the stillness. There is not so much as a movement of a shadow, nor a breeze. We pass the first monastery buildings and slowly walk uphill. The narrow path takes us right up to the Church of the Dormition of the Most Holy Theotokos. To the left of the church there is one building and to the right there are two. A huge cross erected on a nearby rock dominates the scene. One feels an urge to fall down before it in prayer.

History tells us that a mine once stood here, near the village, and that it was destroyed by a flood. Later a group of monks came to live and struggle in the caves that the receding water had left in the rocky hills. The church was built by the Serbian King Milutin and is first mentioned in 1552. The frescoes in the church were painted in 1856, around the time when Djuro Jakshich wrote the "Pilgrimage to Gornjak." During the restoration of the church in the nintenth century, a scroll written in Armenian and Slavonic dating from 1218 was built into the northern wall of the church.

A young man with an embroidered satchel slung over his shoulder has arrived before us. "It's all right, Father, I can wait.... I have plenty of time," we hear him saying as he walks around a wooden table to kiss the hand of an elderly monk, a frail figure with a long white beard. Fr. Thaddeus! We greet him and ask for his blessing. His hand is as cool as this December morning and as soft as his voice. We take our places around the wooden table beneath the vine that has long been bared of its leaves by the autumn winds. From where we are sitting, we can see, as on the palm of a hand, the road, the winding Vitovnica river, and the red path that leads to the monastery gates.

Fr. Thaddeus talks in the rhythm of his breathing: at times he slows down, at times he speaks faster. He pauses between sentences and sometimes drops the ending of a word. It is clear to us that it is a great effort for him to speak.

Fr. Thaddeus' health began to deteriorate severely from excessive conversation and bearing the burdens of many, often to the point of complete exhaustion. His inner peace was disturbed, for, as he would say, "when we pray for someone, we take upon ourselves his suffering." Many years of inner suffering were needed for him to learn how to ease the heavy burden of thoughts that had accumulated over time with the countless confessions he had heard, which he had taken upon himself in an act of self-sacrifice like the good shepherd that he was. "We must learn to ease the burden of thoughts that bears down upon us. As soon as we feel burdened, we must turn to the Lord and give our worries over to Him, as well as the worries and cares of our loved ones. I always give my problems over to the Lord, as well as the problems of those that come to me. I give them over to the Lord and His Most Holy Mother, and they take care of everything. As for me, how can I help others when I cannot even help myself?"

In 1992 he had a heart attack and in 1996 a second. "I had two heart attacks," remembers Fr. Thaddeus, "because of talking too much with people. Five years ago I had a heart attack on the right side; I thought that the end had come, but here I am. I have no strength left in me to talk, but I can serve, I can sing. I should be silent, and spend the rest of my days in stillness. But what can one do? People keep on coming with all their worries and their afflictions. There was a time when I didn't have high blood pressure. Now, when I listen to people's difficulties, these pass on to me—that's why my blood pressure is high. I don't like medication either, but, here we are; I'm still alive!"

Elder Thaddeus' words of instruction to his spiritual children were simple. His face was always radiant and joyful, as his inner peace was reflected in it. "We do not need to say anything or do anything, but we feel so good in the presence of a humble and meek person who is full of love and goodness. He does not have to say anything either, yet he radiates warmth, and it is as though we have caught a chill and have come into a warm and pleasant room and it warms us. You see, that is the meaning of good thoughts, good desires full of love and goodness." Thus spoke the elder about those who possessed a spirit of humility and meekness, and in reality, it was to him that the faithful flocked to warm the chills of their souls under the rays of the Sun of the Kingdom of God, the rays of peace and joy in the Holy Spirit which the elder radiated.

Fr. Thaddeus showed a patristic, simple, and humble approach to everyday matters, as well as to matters pertaining to the Church and her Holy Mysteries. "Love little things," he taught, "and strive for that which is modest and simple. When the soul is mature, God will give it inner peace. The Lord watches over us, and He is pleased that you long for His peace. Until the soul is ready, He will only sometimes allow us to see that He is present everywhere and fills all things. At these moments the soul feels such joy! It feels as though it has everything! But then the Lord conceals Himself from us again, in order that we might long for Him and seek Him with our hearts!" Fr. Thaddeus was always gentle with the weak and suffering, and strict with those who expressed a desire to labor for perfection. However, he was the most strict toward himself.

For Elder Thaddeus, everything in the spiritual life was important. Even the least significant problem of an "ordinary" person was of utmost importance to the elder, for he knew that it was through that particular problem or affliction that the salvation of the person was being decided. That kind of person was most important for Fr. Thaddeus, for, as the Gospel witnesses, ordinary men are most important to God.

Fr. Thaddeus tirelessly taught all the Christian men and

Elder Thaddeus.

women who came to him at Vitovnica the truth of the centuries-old experience of the Church—so easily forgotten and ignored in our day and age—that man is a creature of energy and thought, a being of noetic energies. He taught that most of the thoughts which torment us from the inside are not ours at all, but come from the demons, that every one of us has the God-given power and freedom to refuse such thoughts, and that our lives depend on the quality of the thoughts we nurture in our minds and hearts.

"All things here on this earth," said Fr. Thaddeus, "all that is good and also all that is not, everything comes from our thoughts. Our thoughts determine our whole life. If our thoughts are destructive, we will have no peace. If they are quiet, meek and simple, our life will be the same, and we will have peace within us. It will radiate from us and influence all beings around us—rational beings, animals, and even plants. Such is our 'thought apparatus,' which emits thoughts with which we influence all other beings. And everyone expects peace, consolation, love, and respect from us."

"Not I, but the Lord"

The people flocked to him with their afflictions, pain and doubts, and the elder answered their questions—not by himself and with his own reasoning, but by what God Himself told him. "People come to me with a question they haven't even formulated, and God, of course, knows what their needs are. God, not I. They think I read their thoughts. It is God Who answers them, not I."

Many of Fr. Thaddeus' spiritual children benefited from the elder's clairvoyance. A Serbian abbot related some incidents that revealed the elder's gift of insight. This abbot said that, when he first became superior of his monastery, it was very difficult for him. He had to deal with many problems and fulfill many responsibilities, and he longed to get away from these in order to live a life of undisturbed prayer. He formed a plan to secretly go to Mount Athos, find a remote cell in which to live in silence and prayer, and go under a different name so that people would not know who he was. His desire was to stay for the rest of his life on the Holy Mountain. He told no one about this plan, but formed the firm intention in his mind to carry it out. Then Fr. Thaddeus visited his monastery. With the monastery fathers and brothers assembled, the abbot asked Fr. Thaddeus to speak to everyone about prayer. Fr. Thaddeus then turned to the abbot, and, looking him directly in the eye, said: "When I was a young abbot, I was very disobedient. I formed the desire to leave my responsibilities in Serbia and to live for the rest of my life as a monk on Mount Athos." The abbot then told Fr. Thaddeus that he did not want him to talk on that subject, but instead to tell the assembled brethren about prayer. But Fr. Thaddeus, still looking at the abbot, only repeated what he had said earlier: "When I was a young abbot,

Elder Thaddeus speaking with pilgrims.

I was very disobedient ..." The abbot then had no doubt that Fr. Thaddeus had been given by God to know his secret intention, and that he was giving him direct and personal counsel to abandon this intention and continue carrying out the responsibilities that had been entrusted to him.

At a later time, the same abbot had become very discouraged because many guests were coming to the monastery and were starting to infiltrate the monastic life. "I started to complain to God," he recalls, "asking Him if there was ever in history a monastery like ours, in which lay people played a greater role in monastery life than the brothers. Soon after, Fr. Thaddeus visited the monastery, and he sat in a room with local people, the monks, and a bishop. The bishop asked Fr. Thaddeus to tell us about Miljkovo Monastery and about the saints that were there. Fr. Thaddeus replied that there were some saints there, and then, looking at me said, 'But not only saints—there were also other people there.' And he related a story about how a drunken monk had to be retrieved from the city in a wheelbarrow. He went on to relate many other stories that made me realize that our monastery was undergoing much smaller temptations than Miljkovo." The abbot understood that Fr. Thaddeus had again been informed by God of his secret thought, and had again offered him a direct word of counsel so that he would continue bearing his cross as abbot.

There were also those who approached him in an unhealthy, idolatrous manner: some out of ignorance, others because of their emotional ties to him, and a few with evil intentions. The Elder opposed this strongly, and sometimes, because of events brought about by certain people who posed as his "spiritual children," he suffered a lot. "One must always love God first," he taught. "One's relatives and fellow men come only second after God. We must never be idols to one another, for such is the will of God." However, even the Athonite and Optina Elders were subject to this kind of temptation, because people are always prone to worshipping created matter rather than the Creator Himself. Defending the truth of God-given spiritual fatherhood, Elder Thaddeus said: "A peaceful mind lent modesty to our white-haired and divinely wise holy elders. They never permitted people to address them as though they were idols or deities. That is the huge difference between the real elders of yesteryear and the new, self-made 'psychics' of today."

There were also people who came to Vitovnica with impure intentions. As a rule, they left Vitovnica in the same state of emptiness in which they had come. Elder Thaddeus remembered one such person: "Once, a writer from Belgrade came to see me. He paid for a taxi to bring him here all the way from Belgrade. He wanted me to tell him whether his novels would sell well. I told him I was no psychic.... In the end the writer left, saying that he had made a mistake in coming to see me. You see, he came for strictly materialistic reasons, to learn whether his books would bring him fame and material wealth."

If anyone came to him expecting an instant miracle from a conversation with him, Fr. Thaddeus would tell him with the gentleness of a mother: "You come to me with your problems. I have many problems too, and the Lord comforts us all. I tell you my troubles, you tell me yours, and everything will be well afterwards.... The Lord will have comforted us!"

One of Fr. Thaddeus' many spiritual children related the elder's method of teaching the faithful. "Usually, when I asked Fr. Thaddeus a question, he would give me a brief answer and then say, 'Such-and-such Holy Father has written a lot about this. Shall I go and fetch the book so we can go over it together?' I would always agree eagerly, and he would leaf through the book and find the appropriate passages and read them out loud, stopping at times to add his own comments. I have never met anyone who was so familiar with patristic literature as was Fr. Thaddeus."

Another pilgrim remembers the sobriety, deeply rooted in Church tradition, which Fr. Thaddeus demonstrated during spiritual talks with the faithful. "The Elder never gave direct answers to my very direct questions. He always answered by quoting the Holy Fathers or the Lives of the saints, which is always the only truly correct way of answering questions."

By God's providence, in 1986 one of the elder's spiritual children, M., was permitted to discover that besides the regular monastic labors (fasting, vigils, prostrations), Fr. Thaddeus practiced another form of asceticism: he never lay down on his bed, not even to sleep. By the will of God, M. came into the elder's cell to ask for a blessing to perform some task in the monastery woods and saw the elder sitting on his bed, his back against the wall, and his head bowed on his chest, thus allowing his body to rest. So faithfully did he adhere to his monastic vow of poverty that he possessed nothing material, not even privacy. In the new monastery building, the door on the elder's cell was made out of glass, so that one could see the interior of his cell.

In 1987, pilgrim V. wrote, "Fr. Thaddeus is seventy-three years old. I see no change whatsoever in him: he is gentle and joyful, and always equally accessible, hospitable and restrained with everyone. In a word, he is just what we imagine a Christian should be like."

In the same year the elder told this pilgrim of a recent dream. In this dream, he was in a large church kissing the icons. "Christ Himself appeared before the icon of the Lord. He was weeping. Upon being asked why He was shedding tears, He answered that it was because, when confronted with evil, people fought back with evil."

Once, Fr. Thaddeus shared a meal at Vitovnica with a pious visitor from Belgrade. After the meal, the visitor noticed several bread crumbs in the elder's long beard. When they had both risen from the table, he gently told Fr. Thaddeus that he ought to shake the crumbs from his beard, so that the other visitors would not see them and wonder what kind of monk he was. However, the elder only smiled and said, "It is a pity to throw these crumbs away, when the birds can feast on them!" Then he sat on a bench in the garden, leaned back in his seat, and called to a sparrow sitting on a nearby tree, "Come, little sparrow, come and eat!" The visitor saw with his own eyes how the sparrow flew down and settled on Fr. Thaddeus' beard, pecking at it until it had eaten the last crumb.

With his spiritual eyes set on the Divine mystery of creation and its mystical gratefulness to its Creator, as well as on the terrible mystery of man's abuse of creation and his joyless, materialistic, and destructive misuse of nature, Fr. Thaddeus spoke to the Vitovnica pilgrims in these words: "Life is increasingly being destroyed and extinguished ... That's no mystery! Even some ten years ago when there used to be heavy snowfalls, you could see whole families of rabbits playing in the clearings among the trees at night in the moonlight. They would run around in circles, chasing one another and playing, hundreds of them, turning cartwheels in the snow, playing joyfully. This was joy, the joy of living! The animals have it. Man takes this joy away from them. They have the joy of living, while we have all kinds of material things, yet we are never happy, never satisfied. The animals do not worry about tomorrow, they do not gather wheat into their granaries, yet the Lord feeds them all. They nibble on a root here, find a place to sleep there, and they are grateful to God. Not so we men ..."

In 1998 Fr. Thaddeus came to Belgrade, where he delivered his famous homily entitled "Repentance Is a Change of Life" in the overcrowded "Shumadija" theatre in the Belgrade suburb of Banovo Brdo. This homily was later broadcast many times on several television stations as one of the most significant spiritual events in Belgrade in those difficult times.[1]

"Let Us Be the Sons of Light!"

Fr. Thaddeus spent the last years of his life away from his monastery and diocese, as others girded him and carried him where he did not wish to go (cf. John 21:18). Fr. Thaddeus accepted this of his own free will and resigned himself to a life outside his monastery and his diocese. He moved from place to place, following the model of the One Who from the beginning to the end of His life had no place to lay His head. He spent several months in monasteries in the Metropolitanate of Montenegro and the Littoral, and toward the very end of his earthly life he found refuge in the home of the Grubor family in the city of Bachka Palanka, where he would remain until his falling asleep.

In November 2001, in a conversation with his spiritual children from Belgrade, his health visibly deteriorating but his face already alight with the cloudless clarity of the Kingdom of God, Fr. Thaddeus spoke in a cracked voice, almost a whisper,

[1] See pages 171–81 of this book for the homily.

words which shone with light: "All the Holy Fathers lived a good life, a quiet life. All of them say that the perfection of the Christian life is in extreme humility. This means that patient long-suffering is what we most need in this life. We must bear everything patiently and forgive all. If we have good thoughts and desires, these thoughts will give us peace and joy even in this life, and even more so in eternity. Then we will see that there is no death, that the Lord has vanquished death, and that He has given us eternal life!"

In 2002, His Grace Amphilochius, Metropolitan of Montenegro and the Littoral, visited the ailing Elder Thaddeus in Bachka Palanka. He came to bid farewell and pay his respects to the elder, one of the great Serbian ascetics of the twentieth century.

A stroke and a long illness allowed Fr. Thaddeus to be perfected through the extreme helplessness of his ailment, which he endured until the very end with love, obedience, and humility. Elder Thaddeus of Vitovnica fell asleep in Christ the Savior during the night between March 31/April 13 and April 1/14, 2003 in Bachka Palanka, on the feast day of St. Mary of Egypt, the model of repentance and obedience. On that day the quiet elder of Vitovnica reached the summit of the ladder of obedience to Christ and His Church, and attained the goal he had strived toward all his life—the Heavenly Kingdom.

On April 2/15, 2003, Fr. Thaddeus' funeral was served, and his fellow monastics and spiritual children bade farewell to him with quiet prayers and tears, many having traveled from distant parts of Serbia to be at his burial. His spiritual children were united in sorrow at having lost their father on earth, yet were comforted by the joy of gaining a prayerful intercessor in heaven.

As was the case with many saints of God (St. Cuthbert of Lindisfarne, St. Gerasimus of the Jordan, St. Seraphim of Sarov)—who poured forth the love of God on all living things, drawing them toward themselves—the animals paid their respects at the repose of the God-filled elder. Many species of birds flocked

The funeral of Elder Thaddeus at Vitovnica Monastery.

together and came to bid farewell to the elder who had loved them so much and had always spoken about them with great tenderness:

"They are grateful to God. Not so us men. The birds are always singing praises to the Lord. They begin their song early, at three o'clock in the morning, and don't stop until nine. At nine they calm down a little bit—it's only then that they go looking for food to feed their young. Then they start singing again. Nobody tells them to sing—they just do. And what about us? We're always frowning, always pouting; we don't feel like singing or doing anything else. We should follow the example of the birds. They're always joyful whereas we're always bothered by something. What is it that bothers us? Nothing, really.... Isn't that right?"

A Quiet Witness to the Quiet Savior

As a spiritual father, Elder Thaddeus' service was directed entirely to the salvation of the faithful people of the Church. His labors were comprised exclusively of witnessing to the ascetic and liturgical spirituality of the Church, which is nothing other than the Holy Spirit working in the Body of Christ through the uncreated energies of God for the cleansing, enlightenment, and deification of all who strive for salvation. With the blessing of the Church, a spiritual father leads his spiritual children toward Christ, making them a part of Christ's Body so that, by living a Christian life and taking part in the Holy Mysteries, they might be cured of their fallen state, mortality, and corruption. Thus, it is not the spiritual father who heals them, but the Holy Spirit through the Divine energies, which are unoriginate and were revealed to man through our Lord Jesus Christ, the Incarnate Savior. Man can be spiritually healed, enlightened and deified only by the Living God—the Holy Trinity. However, God does not do this without man's participation, and this mystical synergy is the essence of Orthodox life in the Church.

According to our Church tradition as defined by St. Maximus the Confessor, the three levels of ascetic and mystical perfection are the cleansing from passions (practical philosophy), enlightenment of the *nous*[1] and the heart[2] (natural contemplation), and deification, true communion with the Holy Spirit (mystical theology).[3] During his lifetime, Fr. Thaddeus achieved all three levels in the school of the Holy Spirit. Fr. Thaddeus' acquisition of these perfections was known to all those who met him, talked with him, confessed to him, and received Holy Communion from him. We also know, from his accounts of communication with the angels and saints, modestly narrated in the third person, that the elder had also been made worthy of achieving that most exalted mystical level

---

[1] *Nous:* the highest faculty of the soul which, when purified, can come to a knowledge of God through His energies.

[2] *Heart:* the spiritual center of man's being, connected in some sense with the physical organ of the heart.

[3] Cf. St. Maximus the Confessor, *Various Texts,* 5.94; in *The Philokalia,* vol. 2 (London: Faber and Faber, 1981), p. 283.

The grave of Elder Thaddeus, next to the Dormition Church
in Vitovnica Monastery.

of theology in which, in the words of Metropolitan Hierotheos (Vlachos), "deified man communicates with the angelic powers and is made worthy of beholding uncreated light. Divine depths are revealed to him by the Holy Spirit and he receives the uncreated energy of God. Before such a man are unveiled many mysteries of the Gospel of God which remain hidden from others."

Standing firmly in the Church tradition rooted in *The Philokalia*,[1] Elder Thaddeus witnessed to his contemporaries the experience and living theology of the Holy Fathers in every aspect of man's salvation: "We cannot achieve salvation unless we change our thoughts and make them different.... This is achieved by the work of Divine power in us. Our minds thus become deified, free of passions, and holy. Only a mind which has God within it and a constant remembrance of the Lord can be deified. By knowing that He is in us and we are in Him, we can move around like fish in the water. He is everywhere, and we, like the fish, swim in Him. As soon as we leave Him, we die spiritually."

The life of Elder Thaddeus is woven into Christ's economy and His work of salvation. He thus became a quiet witness to the quiet Savior among the Serbian people in one of the most difficult periods of their history (1914–2003). For the Serbs, this was a time of spiritual and historical cataclysm: two World Wars as well as a civil war, a fifty-year Communist occupation of the country, the wars in Krajina, Bosnia and Hercegovina, the attack of the NATO forces on the people of Serbia in 1999, the occupation of Kosovo and Metohija, and the continuing globalization of societies around the world. In this hour of darkness which has extended to an entire century of war and suffering, Elder Thaddeus searched for peace and joy in the Holy Spirit and witnessed to it, demonstrating by his own example the victory in choosing the narrow path to the Kingdom of God.

---

[1] *The Philokalia*: an anthology of classical ascetical writings of the Holy Fathers compiled by St. Nicodemus of the Holy Mountain and St. Macarius of Corinth.

PART TWO

THE TEACHINGS OF ELDER THADDEUS

Elder Thaddeus.

CHAPTER ONE

ON THOUGHTS

1. Our life depends on the kind of thoughts we nurture. If our thoughts are peaceful, calm, meek, and kind, then that is what our life is like. If our attention is turned to the circumstances in which we live, we are drawn into a whirlpool of thoughts and can have neither peace nor tranquility.

2. Everything, both good and evil, comes from our thoughts. Our thoughts become reality. Even today we can see that all of creation, everything that exists on the earth and in the cosmos, is nothing but Divine thought made material in time and space. We humans were created in the image of God. Mankind was given a great gift, but we hardly understand that. God's energy and life is in us, but we do not realize it. Neither do we understand that we greatly influence others with our thoughts. We can be very good or very evil, depending on the kind of thoughts and desires we breed.

If our thoughts are kind, peaceful, and quiet, turned only toward good, then we also influence ourselves and radiate peace all around us—in our family, in the whole country, everywhere. This is true not only here on earth, but in the cosmos as well. When we labor in the fields of the Lord, we create harmony. Divine harmony, peace, and quiet spread everywhere. However, when we breed negative thoughts, that is a great evil. When there is evil in us, we radiate it among our family members and wherever we go. So you see, we can be very good or very evil. If that's the way it is, it is certainly better to choose good! Destructive thoughts destroy the stillness within, and then we have no peace.

Our starting point is always wrong. Instead of beginning with ourselves, we always want to change others first and ourselves last. If everyone were to begin first with themselves, then there would be peace all around! St. John Chrysostom said that no one can harm the man who does not injure himself—not even the devil.[1] You see, we are the sole architects of our future.

By his thoughts man often disturbs the order of creation. That is how the first people were destroyed—in a flood—because of their evil thoughts and intentions. This is true even today; our thoughts are evil, and therefore we do not bear good fruit. We must change. Each individual must change, but it is unfortunate that we do not have examples to guide us, either in our families or in society.

3. The Old Testament people were unable to accept God's boundless love. Likewise, they were unable to accept His commandments and continued to follow the ancient rule of an eye for an eye and a tooth for a tooth (cf. Ex. 21:24). Even today, we Christians still adhere to this Old Testament rule and are therefore surrounded by evil. We are also surrounded by many unpleasant things in life which destroy our inner peace. We are unable to forgive even our own brother, let alone others.

You can see now how it goes. When we nurture evil thoughts, we become evil. We may think that we are good, but evil is in us. We do not have the strength to resist it. And we know that, as Christians, we must not even think evil, let alone do it.

We, however, have Divine power, Divine life, and Divine energy. On the day of the Final Judgment we shall have to give an answer for the way we have used this Divine power, life, and energy which have been given to us: whether we have contributed to the harmony in the universe, or have sown disharmony.

[1] See St. John Chrysostom, *Treatise to Prove That No One Can Harm the Man Who Does Not Injure Himself;* in *Nicene and Post-Nicene Fathers,* First Series, vol. 9 (Peabody, Mass.: Hendrickson Publishers, 1994), pp. 269–84.

4. The Lord has taken all of our sufferings and cares upon Himself, and He has said that He will provide for all our needs, yet we hold on to our cares so tightly that we create unrest in our hearts and minds, in our families, and all around us.

Whenever I am burdened by problems, and when I try to bear all the cares of the monastery and the brotherhood by myself, then there is trouble in store for me and the brethren. Even the easiest job is carried out with great difficulty. But when I commit myself, the brotherhood, and everything else unto the Lord, even the hardest of jobs gets done with ease. There is no pressure, and peace reigns among the brethren.

5. The Lord is present everywhere, and nothing happens without His will or His permission, either in this life or in eternity. When we accept this idea, everything is made easier. If God would allow us to do everything the way we desire and when we desire, this would certainly result in catastrophe. One cannot even imagine the chaos that would occur. God reminds us in different ways of His presence. We, however, quickly forget about it, especially when things are going well for us. We forget that we are here for a short time only, and we think that we will be around forever, but when misfortune strikes, we cry, "Lord have mercy!" This is why we should try hard to change our character for the better.

6. Once, two women came to me and brought a third who was dragging her leg. She could barely walk. She said that she had been to several doctors, but they were not able to say what was wrong with her. I told her that her nerves were weak. I also told her that mine was a worse case than hers! She said that her husband had left her. "Of course he has," I said. "Who is going to take care of the children, who will prepare his meals for him when you are so depressed? You are not physically ill! You are too depressed. Sing! Sing and your husband will come back to you!" I told her that I was going to the church to read some prayers, and that I wanted

her to go home by herself. She looked at me for a while and then practically ran to the car. The other two were amazed. "She is well," I said, "and she no longer needs your help!"

7. A man who has within him the Kingdom of Heaven radiates holy thoughts, Divine thoughts. The Kingdom of God creates within us an atmosphere of heaven, as opposed to the atmosphere of hell that is radiated by a person when hades abides in his heart. The role of Christians in the world is to filter the atmosphere on earth and expand the atmosphere of the Kingdom of God.

We can keep guard over the whole world by keeping guard over the atmosphere of heaven within us, for if we lose the Kingdom of Heaven, we will save neither ourselves nor others. He who has the Kingdom of God in himself will imperceptibly pass it on to others. People will be attracted by the peace and warmth in us; they will want to be near us, and the atmosphere of heaven will gradually pass on to them. It is not even necessary to speak to people about this. The atmosphere of heaven will radiate from us even when we keep silence or talk about ordinary things. It will radiate from us even though we may not be aware of it.

The Kingdom of God will not make its abode in the heart of a person who has no obedience, for such a person always wants his will—rather than God's—to be done. In the Kingdom of God, there is no possibility of a kingdom within a kingdom. This was the goal of the fallen spirits too, and that is why they have fallen away from the Lord, the King of Glory.

A person who is entrapped in the vicious cycle of chaotic thoughts, in the atmosphere of hades, or has only so much as touched it, feels the torments of hell. For example, we read the newspapers or take a walk in the streets, and afterwards we suddenly feel that something is not quite right in our souls; we feel an emptiness; we feel sadness. That is because by reading all sorts of things, our mind becomes distracted and the atmosphere of hades has free access to our minds.

8. The Holy Fathers tell us to let our attention be on the Lord immediately upon waking, to let our thoughts be united with Him during the entire day, and to remember Him at every moment. The Holy Fathers prayed to be delivered from forgetfulness, for we often get carried away by the things of this world and forget the Lord.... We forget that He is everywhere and that any job we do and any task we perform is His. We think that the job we are doing is for someone else and we often perform our tasks unwillingly. When we perform a task unwillingly, soon resistance and a feeling of disgust are born in us, and then our life becomes filled with resistance and disgust for everything, and we grow old in this manner.

9. Your thoughts are burdened because you are influenced by the thoughts of your fellow men. Pray to the Lord that He might take this burden from you. These are the thoughts of others which differ from yours. They have their plan, and their plan is to attack you with their thoughts. Instead of letting go, you have allowed yourself to become part of their plan, so of course you suffer. Had you ignored the attack, you would have kept your peace. They could have thought or said anything at all about you, yet you would have remained calm and at peace. Soon all their anger would have died down, like a deflated balloon, because of the pure and peaceful thoughts that would have come from you. If you are like that, calm and full of love, if all you think are good and kind thoughts, they will stop warring against you in their thoughts and will not threaten you anymore. But if you demand an eye for an eye, that is war. Where there is war there can be no peace. How can there be peace on a battlefield, when everyone is looking over their shoulders and anticipating a surprise attack from the enemy?

10. The Holy Fathers struggled in acquiring peace. One of the Holy Fathers said, "The mind is a great wanderer. It is always

traveling. It cannot rest until the only One Who can lay it to rest appears." If the Holy Fathers fought so hard to acquire peace, we too must always keep in mind that we must strive to be good all the time. And so, this means that our mind cannot attain peace unless the Mighty One, the Holy Spirit, enlightens us. That is when our minds learn to contemplate in the right way, and we come to the realization that quiet and gentle thoughts, full of love and forgiveness, are the way to peace and stillness.

Why does the Lord command us to love our enemies and to pray for them? Not for their sake, but for ours! For as long as we bear grudges, as long as we dwell on how someone offended us, we will have no peace.

If the head of a family is burdened with cares and worries about the future of his family, he will have no peace. All the members of the family will feel his unrest. They will know that something is wrong, but they will not know exactly what. We can see how much our thoughts influence others. Misunderstandings in the family also happen because of our thoughts.

11. In our town of Petrovac there used to be a priest named Fr. B. He had a distinctive personality—a little rough, sharp-spoken, and demanding in discipline—but he had an unbelievable love for animals. There were always dogs and cats in his house. One autumn day he went to bless the home of a parishioner who had a huge ferocious German shepherd. The dog was as big as a calf. When Fr. B. walked through the gate, the dog leapt forward and threw himself at the priest. Everyone was sure that he was attacking him. But the priest spread his arms wide and said, "Come, let's wrestle!" The dog placed his paws on his shoulders and began to lick his face. Everyone was amazed. "He knows I like animals!" said the priest. This is what happens when a person has good thoughts. When animals, who are not rational beings, feel this, how much more will our fellow men feel our good

thoughts? Our thoughts create either harmony or disharmony in the world.

12. Once a girl came to see me. She was a university student, and both her parents were doctors. She said she had problems with one of her professors, who refused to mark her paper. I told her, "Why do you wage war with your teacher? You should respect her as though she were your mother. She is disciplining you for your own good." The girl would not hear of it. "No, Father," she said. "That teacher is mean—she's like this, she's like that. I give all the right answers to her questions and all she does is tell me to come next time. She hasn't given me a mark yet." I told the girl that her teacher was evidently distracted, but that she was waging a war against her teacher in her mind. I told her that she must pray for her teacher, that the Lord might send an angel of peace, and that He might give her the strength to love her teacher. Then everything would be all right. The girl thought I was telling her fairy tales. This went on for another year, and she began to lose hope of ever completing her first year. Then she began to pray for her teacher, and the next time she sat for an exam she passed and received a high mark.

13. As soon as a desire or a worldly thought enters our mind, God immediately sends a warning. Instead of coming to our senses and blocking such thoughts and desires, we nurture them and long for them, and afterwards we wonder why bad things happen to us. These signs of warning come in the form of temptations.

14. In our minds we conceive everything we do, say, and plan. Without this we cannot do or say anything. Everything first receives its shape and form in the mind; all of our energy is first made manifest in our thoughts. Thoughts are the power that conceives everything in the center of our being (the heart), and

when we are united with the Source of life, everything is revealed to us and we are open to all kinds of knowledge.

15. When a person has the Grace of God, his thoughts are unbelievably powerful, because it is the power of God Himself that acts in us. If we have turned away from God in our thoughts and hearts, then our thoughts can be terrible, even death-dealing, to our fellow men. If we are united with the Lord with a heart full of faith, the power of Grace works in us. But if we have not yet cleansed ourselves from pride and still feel offended and angered when others say unkind words to us, then the power of God in us is diminishing.

16. An old woman came to me and told me that her neighbor was bothering her. She said the other woman was constantly throwing things into her yard, so she was at her wits' end. I asked her why she was always quarreling with her neighbor. But the old woman said that she never even spoke to her evil neighbor. I insisted that she quarreled with her every day. I said to her, "You are convinced that she is doing evil things to you, and you are constantly thinking about her. Let her do whatever it is she is doing; you just turn your thoughts to prayer, and you will see that it will stop bothering you."

17. The Apostle James says, "You say you have faith; show your faith through your works, then" (cf. James 2:18). Satan, too, believes and trembles (cf. James 2:19), yet he opposes God and every good thing. Many people on this earth consider themselves to be atheists, but when we think carefully we understand that there is no rational being on the planet Earth who does not long after true life and absolute love. Absolute love never changes; it lasts forever. We long for absolute good and absolute peace with all our heart. In reality, we long for God. God is life, God is love; He is peace and joy. In our hearts we long for God, but in our thoughts

we oppose Him. As we said, Satan believes and trembles, yet he opposes God. Likewise, an atheist is not really an atheist, but an opponent of God.

Thus, we long after God in our hearts but oppose Him in our thoughts. Our opposition cannot harm God, for He is Almighty, but it can certainly harm us. Our thoughts, moods, and desires set a path for our life. Our thoughts reflect our whole life. If our thoughts are quiet, peaceful, and full of love, kindness, and purity, then we have peace, for peaceful thoughts make possible the existence of inner peace, which radiates from us. However, if we breed negative thoughts, then our inner peace is shattered.

Here is what the Holy Fathers say about thoughts: "If thoughts that take away our peace assail us, know that they are from hell." Such thoughts must not be accepted. They must be banished immediately. We must struggle for our own good and strive for peace to take root in our souls—peace, joy, and Divine love. Our Heavenly Father wants all of His children to have His Divine properties. He wants us to be full of love, peace, joy, truthfulness, and kindness. He wants us to be able to comfort others. We also want to become meek and humble, for only such a person radiates goodness and kindness.... Such a person is never insulted even when you shout and scold him; you can even hit him and all he does is pity you for tormenting yourself so. There are very few such people on this earth, but they are the reason why the sun still warms planet Earth and why God gives us His blessing to go on living and to have everything we need in order to live. You see now why our thoughts must change.

18. We have very little faith in the Lord, very little trust. If we trusted the Lord as much as we trust a friend when we ask him to do something for us, neither we as individuals nor our whole country would suffer so much. The chaos in our minds and in our whole country comes from our thoughts. We are the ones creating the disharmony of thoughts, and if our politicians were

of one thought and one mind, things would not be like this. We are not aware that we have Divine energy in us, Divine life. The uniting of each individual with others—since we all possess this energy—creates a great power and the enemy flees from it, because here is harmony.

19. Thoughts are planted in our minds all the time, from all sides and directions. Were it given us to see the radii of thoughts, we would see a real net of thoughts. Everyone has a "receiver" in his mind, one that is much more precise and sophisticated than a radio or a television set. How wonderful is the mind of man! Unfortunately, we do not appreciate this. We do not know how to unite ourselves with the Source of life and to feel joy. The adversary is always planting seeds in our minds. St. Anthony was permitted to see the nets of thoughts around him, and when he saw them, he exclaimed, "Lord, who can be saved?" And he heard a voice saying, "Only those who are meek and humble of heart." The evil spirits cannot touch those who are meek and humble of heart, for they are united with peace and silence. They have no negative thoughts.

20. There is a spiritual child of mine I would like to tell you about. He is a layman, but lives a holier life than many monks. I always tell him, "Do not accept suggestions. Tell yourself, I will not think about this! You will see, you will become well versed in this." And he did. He would refuse the suggestions that came from his thoughts without even going into battle. He has peace. He is physically a very powerful man, who weighs over 220 pounds. But he has peace!

After he had completed his service in the army, his parents wanted him to get married. But he said to me, "I don't know, Father. Seems to me I have become like a eunuch." I told him that of course he did not have to, but again warned him not to accept any suggestions that came from his thoughts, because bodily passions cannot be ignited without the "movie" that our thoughts play and without our watching that "film." The body is at peace when there are no such thoughts. I told him, "Be careful lest you start accepting the proposals from your thoughts. If you do, you will soon see that you have not become a eunuch."

"They want me to get married and I do not wish to," he said. He was at peace and girls did not interest him. One day, he decided to try to accept a suggestion to watch a "movie." He came to me saying, "What do I do now, Father? I can't get it out of my head!" I said to him, "Do you now see how dangerous this is? Now you must be very vigilant in your prayers, and even your knees should smart a little. Everything will be all right after that." Soon he came back again and told me that he was never going to play with fire again. You see, he has acquired this discipline of thoughts, and he is at peace. Now he wants his friends, who engage in all sorts of unseemly behavior, to be chaste, like him. He tells them to either live in chastity or get married. He talks to them about chastity and the Christian life so much that I had to tell him to tone it down a little, for when a person attempts to pull another away from evil deeds, then the demons attack him relentlessly. And attack him they did. He fought many spiritual battles, and the demons physically attacked him. He would come to me all bruised and beaten—it was unbelievable.

This is how we must live—controlling our thoughts. It is not good to dwell on every thought that comes to us; otherwise we lose our peace. If we learn to refuse such proposals, we are quiet. We do not fantasize or create any images in our mind.

21. While praying, a person should not have any thoughts, but rather become selfless. Even the Holy Fathers say this: "While at prayer, behave as though there were no one else in the world, just you and God." When praying, we should not be preoccupied with ourselves, because in that case we are so absorbed in our own needs that we ourselves are detrimental to our prayer. We interfere with

our own prayer. We are our own obstacle. We often think that evil is somewhere out there, but if it were not for the evil that already exists in us, the evil "out there" would not be able to touch us. The evil is in us. However, this evil itself is not to blame. We are to blame for having let it into our hearts and for having disturbed our peace. Let us say someone is threatening us, or trying to talk us into doing something bad. Let him do so; this person has a will of his own. Let him do his job, and we will do ours, which is to preserve our inner peace.

CHAPTER TWO

ON FAMILY LIFE

1. Obedience is constructive, and self-will is destructive. A child should learn to be obedient to his parents as to God. He will remember his parents' words during his entire life and will always respect his elders, and not only elders but even those younger than he is. He will be kind and attentive to everyone. Unfortunately, there are very few families who bring up their children like that.

2. The spirits of evil interfere with children's minds ... and try to disturb them. A child should be taught obedience, especially before the fifth year, because that is the period in which a child's character develops. In this manner, learned character traits remain for the rest of the child's life. Parents should teach their children absolute obedience during that period. When a parent says something, the answer should be, "Amen." But today, unfortunately, parents do not know this and teach their children quite the opposite. And so they grow up ...

3. If the parents say, "Stay here," then the child must stay where they told him. But a child is a child; he cannot sit still in one place. What usually happens is that the parents spank the child for being disobedient. But that is not a good manner of teaching a child obedience. Maybe sometimes a spanking is called for, but then it should be out of love, and the child must feel love. Parents should never spank their children when provoked by anger. For if you are going to correct someone when you are angry, you will achieve nothing. You will only hurt both the person and yourself.

If you want to bring someone onto the right path, to teach and advise him, then you must humble yourself first and talk to the person with a lot of love. He will accept your advice, for he will feel that it is given with love. But when you want to have your way at all costs, then you will achieve nothing. That is how resistance builds up in the child. When a child is disobedient, spanking is not a solution.

4. I read in *Elixir*, a medical journal, that a psychiatrist has said that tears are worth more than thirty tranquilizer tablets. They work better than medication to calm the nerves. Tears are very beneficial for adults, but also for children. After a good cry, a child usually calms down.

5. In 1936 I stayed with a family in Belgrade. Actually, they were of German origin. The husband was German, and the wife was German or Slovenian. They had a little child who was two years old at the time. He still hadn't learned to walk. She would put him on the bed, stomach down, and he would cry. And I told her, "Why don't you hold him for a little while? He'll feel comforted in your arms." And the woman said, "Oh, no. I don't want him to get used to being held, because then he'll want me to hold him all the time and I won't be able to do any work." And she also said, "Crying is good for his lungs; the more he cries, the stronger they will become. He'll stop crying." And that's how it was. He cried for a while and then stopped. He played for a while, then cried a little again, and stopped. Other mothers take their children in their arms as soon as they start to whimper and spoil them.

I remembered how it was when I was a child. I was very sickly and underdeveloped, so they were always holding me in their arms and carrying me about. I couldn't eat any fried food until I was twelve. I fasted all the time and they didn't know what to do with me! My grandmother scolded me when she was nervous, but I still couldn't eat. Then my mother would start offering me other things, and this really bothered me. Too much attention irritates children. Children should know that their parents love them, but the parents should not smother their children with love. A child must be taught to get ready for life, as well as for the Kingdom of Heaven. He must learn how to be a child of light.

6. Eight years ago, a man came to me, visibly sad. His eyes were full of tears. "What is it?" I asked him. The man had two sons. One of them, a student of medicine, had stopped going to the lectures at his school for the past two years. There was not a spark of joy in him; his will to live was gone. The boy was totally confused. I told him not to worry and to take his son for a run on Avala Mountain near Belgrade every day, especially during the week, when few people are there. The boy was just very tired and exhausted from all the pressure at school. The father asked if he should bring the boy to me but I said it was not necessary. I said we would talk when I came to Belgrade.

We met one day in front of the St. George Church in the Belgrade suburb of Banovo Brdo. The boy was feeling very well, and there was no trace of his previous listlessness and apathy. His body needed oxygen in order to feed the brain.

7. Just this morning, a woman came with her son. She has been here before, always complaining about her daughter-in-law. I told her, "Your daughter-in-law is young. She does not yet understand that she must love her mother-in-law as her own mother. But you are older, and you must think about all this."

It is quite a common thing in this world for women to dislike their daughters-in-law, even though they are very good girls. Perhaps she doesn't show it, but a mother-in-law is usually dissatisfied with her daughter-in-law. And the daughter-in-law does not know that she must pray for her mother-in-law, that He send her an angel to guide her steps and also that He give her strength to love her mother-in-law. Instead, she reacts to her mother-in-law's thoughts and the war begins.

You see, every physical war first begins with thoughts. First people cannot stand each other; then they begin destroying one another. Anyway, this poor woman could not understand what I was trying to tell her. I could see that she was very hurt and sad, so I had to spend quite a lot of time with her. I told her, "Give it a try, if nothing else. When your daughter-in-law behaves badly toward you, ask the Lord to send her an angel to guide her, and also ask Him not to forget you. Ask Him to take away this burden from you so that you may not have negative thoughts toward your daughter-in-law, and not only toward her, but also toward anyone who has ever offended you. Pray to Him that He may give you strength to love everyone. And when your thoughts become quiet and peaceful, you will see how things change around you. Your daughter-in-law will change, too. Do you know that you are actually hurting her physically, as though you were beating her? You are doing this all the time. You do not need to hit her physically. It is enough that you cannot stand the thought of her. When this is so, there is no peace in your home. And your son, her husband—he has no peace either. Try to love her. It's difficult, I know ... But do you know why you do not like her?" I asked. "No," she answered. "Well, it is because she took your son away from you. He is not yours anymore, like when he was a little boy. It is natural for a man to cleave to his wife. A mother wants her son to get married and rejoices when he does. But she is the one who suffers most afterwards. Now the son is oriented toward his wife. He is no longer as attentive to his mother as he used to be. That is when the war of thoughts begins. You can fight this war forever, but in the end you will lose. Try to do as I have told you, and you will see how things will change very quickly."

8. Our young people have also been contaminated, especially the children of intellectuals. They [the intellectuals] do not have

enough time to spend with their children, and as a result the children become very self-willed.

I was born prematurely and was underdeveloped as an infant. I could not eat; my mother nursed me until I was three years old. Later, I could not eat fried foods. Even today I do not like to drink milk or eat eggs. But my parents had a hard time keeping me away from sweets. I only stopped eating sweets when I was about twenty-two years old, because I was overdoing it with sweets. Today I can have a bite of something sweet now and then, but it does not attract me as it did before.

It is a problem when a child wants this and that and when his parents cater to his every whim. Then, when the children grow up, they still expect everyone to comply with their wishes. Have you ever seen anything like that? Not even kings and queens get this kind of treatment!

The children of intellectuals whose every wish was fulfilled by their parents when they were young don't know what they want anymore, so in the end many become Satanists. They have already tried everything, and now they openly serve Satan! Many of them even commit suicide—may God preserve us from this terrible sin! Since they are not able to live their lives, they cannot take care of others and have their own families. We cannot hope that they will have a good future.

9. How do our parents know whether we are good children and love them? If they see that we respect and obey their words.

10. Parents scold their children for every little thing. It is as if they do not know how to talk to them kindly and quietly. When a parent needs to discipline a child, the child must feel that behind the strictness there is love. It is a great mistake to punish children as soon as they do something wrong, for nothing is achieved that way. We must first calm down and then, with a lot of love, tell the child that he has done something wrong and

that he must receive some kind of punishment. If the same thing happens again, the child gets a more severe punishment and that is how he learns.

11. There was an old lady, a grandmother, who used to come to me regularly in the 1980s. She told me that her son and daughter-in-law criticized her for going to church. She asked me what to do. "You must preserve peace in your home and in your family at all costs," I told her. "No one can expel the Lord from your heart, for He is always there. A person speaks more eloquently with his actions and with his life than with words."

12. God's Divine will works on us through our parents or through our teachers or employers. If we need to correct a child's behavior, we must do so with much love and attentiveness. If we only so much as think about changing the child's life, we are already dealing him a blow with our thoughts. I have noticed this in my many years as abbot. Many times I would see a brother not behaving properly, and as soon as I would think about correcting him, I would feel that I was dealing him a blow!

Our thoughts can be very penetrating, and they have great power. This is especially true of the thoughts of parents. A parent must bear much and forgive all. We can help others only if we have good and kind thoughts. If we have thoughts about correcting the faults of others, that is like hitting them. No matter how close a person is to us, he will slip away from us because we have dealt him a blow with our thoughts. And we believe that thoughts are nothing!

13. Often there is no unity or oneness of mind in our families because wives and mothers transgress the commandment of obedience to their husbands. God wants married people to be of one mind. By disobeying God's commandment they create an atmosphere of hades in their homes.

14. It is of great significance if there is a person who truly prays in a family. Prayer attracts God's Grace and all the members of the family feel it, even those whose hearts have grown cold. Pray always.

15. You can see for yourself how one can create either harmony or disharmony within the family, depending on the kind of thoughts and wishes one has. If the head of the family is laden with worries and thoughts about some difficulty, then the peace in that family is disturbed. All the members of the family are depressed; they have no peace, no comfort. The head of a family must radiate goodness to all the members of his family. That is how our "thought machine" works.

When I was young I did not know that we must never think negative thoughts about our biological or spiritual parents. We must never hurt them, even in our thoughts. At that time I did not know that insulting others has such negative consequences for all of us. I have suffered much for having hurt my father in my thoughts, and I cannot repent enough for this. My father was a quiet and meek man, unbelievably kind to everyone. Never in his life had he been sick, because he was always at peace and his inner organs functioned without stress. He looked upon his entire life as though it were on film. When someone insulted him he never took it to heart—he was a quiet and meek man. I would have been happy to have inherited his character.

16. Once a girl came to see me. Her father and mother were both doctors. She came to Vitovnica and asked me about many things. She loved her father very much but not her mother. When I asked her why, she answered that her mother had always wanted a son.... I begged her not to wage war against her mother, who had nurtured her in her womb, given her birth, and raised her.... Now this girl is her mother's only comfort in life. Twice she had run away to a monastery, but her father had brought her back home. I told her

not to sadden her parents and to have patience, for one can be a monastic even without a ryassa.[1] The Lord does not require us to wear a ryassa—He wants us to be good and kind.

17. We chastise our children, but we really have no right to do so, because we have failed to teach them the proper way. A woman doctor wrote to me some time ago, saying, "My husband, who is also a medical doctor, and I have one son. Our son has already wrecked three cars—thank God he is still alive. He wants us to buy him another car now, but we just do not have the means. When we come home from work, he tries to take money from us by force. What can I do to solve this problem?" I told her that there is no one to blame but them. They had one son and they granted his every whim from his earliest childhood. When he was younger, his demands were small, but now that he has grown—so have his demands. The only thing they can do now is dedicate a lot of love and a lot of care to their son, so that he might come to his senses and realize that his parents have only his interests in mind. There is no other way but the way of love. You can see by this example how we can improve our life and the lives of those close to us with our thoughts. It is my wish that you succeed in this.

18. Do you see how great is the power of both biological and spiritual parents? I have many times seen the predictions of biological and spiritual parents come true in the lives of their offspring.

Once I was stunned to learn how a certain pious couple killed their son with their thoughts. Their only son was a pious child who had been brought up in the Faith since early childhood. He was like an angel and possessed a goodness that is hard to believe. Once a girl from his town came to ask for his help. The case was this: she had become pregnant by someone, and she wanted

---

[1] *Ryassa:* an outer garment with long sleeves, worn by tonsured monastics, especially during church services.

this young man to marry her because her parents and brothers were very strict. Once her pregnancy started to show, her only solution would be to kill herself. The young man agreed to sign this marriage pact. They agreed that after the child was born and had learned to walk, they would go their separate ways. As this was a very small town this quickly became public knowledge, and the mother of the young man could not bear the shame. The father, on the other hand, said that this was the young man's life, not the mother's, but the mother would not hear of it. "I do not want to set eyes on him alive!" she would say. And this is exactly what happened. Some time later the son was killed in a motorcycle crash. The distraught mother came to me afterwards. "You yourself killed your son," I told her. "A person's thoughts are very powerful. You said that you did not wish to see him alive, and this is what happened." Sometimes our parents are wrong, but for us, their children, they are right, and we must obey them. Then their blessing will be upon us.

19. It is obvious that all doors open to those who have love. Even in the midst of wars where lives are lost all the time, the Lord miraculously preserves those who love their parents, both spiritual and biological. If we had this kind of love for our parents, the world would not be the way it is now. All we can do now is pray, and the Lord will help us and give us strength.

20. The Lord opens the way for us. He reveals His will to us. His will is often revealed to us through our parents. If we obey our parents, everything will be well and we will be blessed, but if we oppose them, then things will not be good for us. Life will go on, but mostly backwards. For instance, you fall in love with a girl and want to marry her, but your parents advise you against it, saying that she is not for you. They offer to find you another girl. But you won't hear of it; the devil has enslaved you, and you will not listen to anyone's advice. So you go and marry the girl, and at first

everything is ideal. Then, after some time, you become fed up with each other; the relationship has died.

The best marriages are those that parents have arranged for their children and when the age difference between the man and the woman is not too great. The couple has no plans; they enter into a marriage union with the blessing of their parents and everything goes well. Marriage is no bed of roses! On the contrary, it is a bitter life. In marriage, you are harnessed to a plough and you must pull, and the blows keep coming. The children need your care. You must provide for them. You must pull the plough, whether you want to or not. When you were single, you thought otherwise. Now you have to think not only for yourself, but for others, too.

21. There were two brothers whose mother was a good and kind woman, who always told them to respect their father, although he was not exactly a good father to them. That was the way to obtain God's blessing, she said. They are grown men now, and they will not permit anyone to say a bad word about their father. They had a difficult childhood, but they had God's blessing and they are full of life. They are very thankful to God.

It was through our parents that God gave us the gift of life. They will have to give an answer for their own behavior; we will not answer for them. What we will have to give an answer for is whether we respected them or not. The situation in our families is very bad because even little children now oppose their parents and talk back to them. That is why things are going so badly for us—the young do not respect their parents anymore. And it is the same situation everywhere in the world.

22. One of Fr. Thaddeus' visitors recounted: "An old lady asked Fr. Thaddeus what she was to do in order that her grandchildren might become pious.

"Fr. Thaddeus replied, 'Let their grandmother always be meek and good; let her never be angry and always be happy. Let her obey everyone, since no one will obey her. Perhaps the grandchildren will not become pious, but one day they will remember their grandmother, and the memory of her will make them better people.'"

23. Because of the Fall of man, the natural order of things has become chaotic. In nature, there is an order for all things, but with man there is chaos. Everything is distorted and turned around. Because of our disobedience to the commandments of our Heavenly Father, we have lost the natural order. In order to reestablish this order, we must practice abstinence.

Abstinence is for everyone, not just for monks. Husbands and wives for whom marriage means only the satisfaction of bodily passions will not be justified. They will answer before God for not having been abstinent. Of course, as the Apostle says, they are not to abstain from each other for a long time, lest the devil deceive them, but they should abstain according to mutual consent (cf. I Cor. 7:1–6). Married people should abstain from corporeal relations during fasts and on great Feast days.

24. One can easily turn heaven into hell. There was an interesting case that happened a few years ago. A married couple came to me. It was clear that God had endowed them with great beauty; I had never seen a more handsome couple. The weather was cold and we served Liturgy in the chapel. When the service was over, they wanted to talk to me. "We have some problems," they said. I heard them out. The case was that they had married each other out of love and had lived peacefully in harmony for a few years. The atmosphere in their family was akin to heaven. Then, recently, they had begun to quarrel over every little thing; there was no more peace in their family. What was worse was that they had a little son, six years old. The child was the reason they had come to me in the first place. They said that the child had totally alienated

himself from them and did not even want to talk to them. He only wanted to be with his grandparents. "We buy him everything he wants, but he is always silent. We buy him toys, clothes, and candy, and he just grabs it from us, tears it apart, or kicks it. Then he goes to his grandparents, leaving us alone. We don't know what to do. Otherwise, he is a healthy and normal child. He doesn't want anything to do with us, his father and his mother. Why is all this happening?" I told them that the child obviously did not want such parents. He was constantly searching for his mommy and daddy, but they were never there. "You used to be happy because you had your parents' blessing," I told them. "Your parents had nothing against your union; on the contrary, they had arranged your marriage even before you had seen each other. So you had your parents' blessing, you married out of love, and there was peace in your union. Your home was like paradise. Now everything has gone wrong—because of your thoughts. Until recently you were satisfied with what you had, you did not fantasize; but now you look at other women with lust, and you give your heart to these women. Your wife looks at other men and gives them her heart. Now you come together in the flesh only, but not in the spirit. Your minds are wandering in different directions. Thank God that you have not stepped outside the boundaries of your marriage vows. Your child senses all of this and he does not want such parents, because not only have you strayed away from each other, you have also alienated yourselves from him. You yourselves have created hell in your home with your thoughts.... It is very painful to have a mother and a father yet not have them. Come back to each other," I told them, "and be as you used to be. Then everything will be good again."

CHAPTER THREE

ON HUMILITY

1. I was very keen to learn what the life of those who served God wholeheartedly was like. So, when I was younger, I liked to leaf through the works of the Holy Fathers, and I saw their inner state. They themselves described this. You see, we only live life on the outside, and we see the stream of life passing by. However, the inner life of every individual is not the same.

I had a desire to learn about the inner life of those who had lived a perfect life here on earth and who were glorified by God both here and in eternity. It was then that I realized, as the Holy Fathers themselves explained, that the perfection of the Christian life consists in extreme humility.

2. One should preach not from one's rational mind but rather from the heart. Only that which is from the heart can touch another heart. One must never attack or oppose anyone. If he who preaches must tell people to keep away from a certain kind of evil, he must do so meekly and humbly, with fear of God.

3. We must suffer much in our hearts until we learn humility. The Lord is ever standing by our side, allowing us to feel pain beneath our left rib so that all the stench can come out. And all we say is, "So-and-so has offended me straight through the heart; this cannot be forgiven!" How can we not forgive, when we are the same as they are? How many times have we offended our fellow men? Well, we must learn to keep our peace. Until you have suffered much in your heart, you cannot learn humility.

The Holy Fathers say that, unless we humble ourselves, the Lord will not stop humbling us. He will use someone in order to humble us. Someone will provoke our anger and do it until we learn to remain calm and peaceful when provoked. When we can stay calm when someone attacks us from all sides, when we can keep our inner peace in spite of that person's rudeness, then our soul will become meek and humble and we will live this life with a full understanding of it. And our neighbors will tell us, "You have changed; you used to have a fiery temperament, but now you have somehow become calm and dispassionate." But we have not become dispassionate. Rather, this is how the victory over evil manifests itself.

4. Man is a great mystery. We often marvel at this mystery and wonder how it is that our bodies function without our willing it. There is no institution or organization on this whole planet that can function as perfectly as the human body.

God is a mystery to all beings. God is in us, and that is why we are a mystery to our own selves. God reveals Himself only to the meek and humble. He is present everywhere, and He is a mystery. We may learn a little about Him, or may gather some knowledge from nature, but for the most part, we are surrounded by mystery.

When a person is meek and humble, he will advance in knowledge.

5. Look at us: as soon as our mood changes, we no longer speak kindly to our fellow men, but instead we answer them sharply. We only make things worse by doing this. When we are dissatisfied, the whole atmosphere between us becomes sour, and we start to offend one another. No matter what people do or say to us, we must be meek and forgive every offense.

6. We think we know a lot, but what we know is very little.

Even those who have striven all their lives to bring progress to mankind—learned scientists and highly educated people—all realize in the end that all their knowledge is but a grain of sand on the seashore. All our achievements are insufficient.

7. Humility is a Divine property and the perfection of the Christian life. It is attained through obedience. He who is not obedient cannot attain humility. There are very few in the world today who have obedience. Our humility is in proportion to our obedience.

Physical, outward humility is easier to attain than inner humility, humility of the mind. That is a special gift. Our holy Father Symeon says that a person who has attained humility of the mind cannot be hurt by anything in the world.[1] Whatever happens, such a person is always at peace. This is truly a Divine property.

Pride, too, has its levels, just like humility. Outward pride is easier to cure, but pride of the mind is almost impossible to eradicate. No one can prove to such a person that he is on the wrong track. But outward pride is curable, because one can go from riches to rags in the twinkling of an eye and become humble whether he wants to or not!

8. Meekness means having a heart that is humbled and peaceful. Children are meek. This is why the Lord says, "If you do not become as children, you shall not enter the Kingdom of Heaven" (cf. Matt. 18:3). A proud person is never satisfied; everything bothers him, and he follows his own will. We must be obedient to the will of God in order to learn humility and meekness while we are still in this life, while there is still time. A heart that is full of love thinks not of itself, but of others. It prays for all living things and for the whole world.

[1] Cf. St. Symeon the New Theologian, *Catechetical Discourses* 31, in *Symeon the New Theologian: The Discourses* (New York: Paulist Press, 1980), p. 330.

9. The Holy Fathers say that he who is born meek has already received his reward, but his reward will not be as great as that of the man who was born with a quick temper and who has learned meekness through humility. Such a person will receive a great reward indeed.

10. QUESTION: How can we consider created matter to be better than us if God has endowed us with a rational mind and has called us His sons?

ANSWER: If you place your hand over your heart and are entirely sincere with yourself, you will realize that you are indeed less than many created things. Look at the bee, how diligently it labors! It gives of itself without reserve, unsparingly. The lifespan of a bee is a month and a half at the most. It often dies working, without going back to its home, the hive. And we? How we pity ourselves and spare ourselves! Or, look at the ant who is never tired of dragging a heavy burden. Even when its burden falls down, the ant patiently picks it up and goes on with its work. As for us, we give up immediately if things do not go the way we want them to!

CHAPTER FOUR

ON SERVING GOD AND NEIGHBOR

1. Even as a child I greatly desired to serve God. Even then I knew that here on earth everything was some kind of service. Parents attend to their children and children attend to their parents. Everyone serves someone else. That was when I decided that I wanted to serve God. Since He is the Parent of all mankind and the entire universe, one should serve Him Who is the greatest of all. As a young child I very much wanted to do that. When I grew older, I knew I could not tell my parents—they would never have given me their blessing—but when I came of age I went to a monastery.

My mother had fallen asleep in the Lord a long time before that, but my father was still living and he objected. Even so, when I told him of my wish to receive the monastic tonsure, I asked his blessing. Thank God, my father gave me his blessing.

2. We should defend one another, for we are brothers—especially we who are of one Faith. There is an example of this in history. Once, when an official delegation of Constantinopolitan dignitaries was sent to the Saracens to negotiate peace, the Saracens argued that Christians disobeyed God's commandment. They said: "Why do you Christians disobey Christ's commandment to love your enemies, but instead persecute and kill us?"

Now, a certain Cyril was part of this delegation. His answer to the Saracens was: "If, in a certain law, there are two commandments that must be fulfilled, which man shall be more righteous, he who fulfills both commandments or he who fulfills only one of them?" The Saracens answered, "He that fulfills both, of course." Then Cyril said, "As individuals we forgive our enemies, but as a community we lay down our lives for one another. For the Lord has said that there is no greater love than to lay down one's life for one's neighbor. As a community we protect one another and lay down our lives for one another. Not only is your aim to enslave us physically, you also aspire to enslave us spiritually. It is for this reason that we defend ourselves. This, therefore, is justified."

Then there is also the example of St. Ioannicius the Great. He was a soldier for twenty years. He was amazing—whenever he fought a battle, he won. He had never been defeated. He never gave a thought to his own life but laid down his own for others. And the Lord preserved him. Later, when he became a monk, he was a great saint and wonderworker. There were many such holy warriors. The Holy King David says: *Blessed are they whose iniquities are forgiven, and whose sins are covered* (Ps. 31:1). Righteousness acts never in its own interest, but in the interest of fellow men.

3. Any work we do here on earth is God's work. However, we always work with reservation, without sincerity. Not only can God not bear that, but no human being can. We know that the universe belongs to God, that the Earth is God's planet, and that everything belongs to God, no matter what type of work we do.

Whether a person is good or not, pious or not, a dedicated worker or not, he will answer for it. We should not think too much about who our superiors are, or who our employer is. What we should bear in mind is that every type of work on earth and in all the universe is God's work, and as such it should be performed from the heart, without reservation. When we do so, we can free ourselves from our interior resistance. Every action of ours will then help our neighbor, beginning with our family, wherever we may be. So we must always be sincere. Then we radiate peace, quiet, and love, and we are loved in return. With our thoughts we either attract or repel enemies, friends, family, and neighbors. However, people usually take this lightly and suffer a lot as a result.

4. Strictness toward our neighbor is dangerous. The strict can progress to a certain point only, and they remain merely at the level of physical abstinence. One must be kind, meek, and merciful in one's relationships with people.

5. If in each family there were just one person who served God zealously, what harmony there would be in the world! I often remember the story of Sister J. She used to come and talk to me often while I was still at the Tumane Monastery. Once she came, together with an organized group of pilgrims, and complained, saying, "I can't bear this any longer! People are so unkind to each other!" She went on to say that she was going to look for another job. I advised her against it, as there were few jobs and a high level of unemployment. I told her to stop the war she was fighting with her colleagues. "But I'm not fighting with anyone!" she said. I explained that, although she was not fighting physically, she was waging war on her colleagues in her thoughts by being dissatisfied with her position. She argued that it was beyond anyone's endurance. "Of course it is," I told her, "but you can't do it yourself. You need God's help. No one knows whether you are praying or not while you are at work. So, when they start offending you, do not return their offences either with words or with negative thoughts. Try not to offend them even in your thoughts; pray to God that He may send them an angel of peace. Also ask that He not forget you. You will not be able to do this immediately, but if you always pray like that, you will see how things will change over time and how the people will change as well. In fact, you are going to change, too." At that time I did not know whether she was going to heed my advice.

This happened in the Tumane Monastery in 1980. In 1981 I was sent to the Vitovnica Monastery. I was standing underneath the quince tree when I noticed a group of pilgrims that had arrived. She was in the group and she came up to me to receive a blessing. And this is what she said to me, "Oh, Father, I had no idea that people were so good!" I asked her whether she was referring to her colleagues at work and she said she was. "They have changed so much, Father, it's unbelievable! No one offends me anymore, and I can see the change in myself, as well." I asked her whether she was at peace with everyone, and she answered that there was one person with whom she could not make peace for a long time. Then, as she read the Gospels, she came to the part where the Lord commands us to love our enemies. Then she said to herself, "You are going to love this person whether you want to or not, because this is what the Lord commands us to do." And now, you see, they are best friends!

If there were just one such person in every company, factory or office! That would be the way toward peace. Only one person who is prayerfully connected to God is needed, and we will have peace everywhere—in the family, at work, in the government, and everywhere. It is in the presence of such a person that we are freed from gloomy and cumbersome thoughts.

6. When we talk to our fellow men and they tell us about their troubles, we will listen to them carefully if we have love for them. We will have compassion for their suffering and pain, for we are God's creatures; we are a manifestation of the love of God. However, we often consider this a great burden, for we are oppressed by our own cares, worries, and weaknesses. We need to rest from all these cares, but only God can give us rest. He is the Bearer of all our infirmities and weaknesses. That is why we must always turn to Him in prayer. That is our only source of comfort. Then we will be relieved of our burdens and the burdens of our neighbors' troubles as well, for we will have taken all of them to the Lord.

As we take more concern for our neighbors' cares and problems, they soon become our own. And our thoughts immediately become occupied with them.

If we listen to our neighbor with only half our attention, of course we will not be able to answer them or comfort them.... We are distracted. They talk, but we do not participate in the conversation; we are immersed in our own thoughts. But if we give them our full attention, then we take up both our own burden and theirs.

7. If we have a burden beyond our bearing, we must turn to the Lord immediately, like this: "O Lord, I cannot even bear my own infirmities, yet now I must bear the burden of so-and-so. I cannot cope with all this responsibility. I cannot do this myself, and, because I feel that I have no desire to cope either, all this weighs even more heavily on my conscience. I wish to help my fellow man, but I don't have the means. My neighbors think that I don't want to help, and that is an additional burden to me."

When we pray to the Lord from our heart and bring all our cares and troubles to Him—as well as the cares and troubles of our fellow men—He takes this burden from us, and we feel lighter immediately. Whereas before we were entangled in the net of our own thoughts, now we are relaxed and at peace, for we have given everything over to the Lord. If we do not learn to do this, then we will become more and more burdened each day, and there will come a time when we will not even be able to talk to our fellow men. Why? Because we are overstressed. And we think to ourselves, "Go away! I can barely cope with my own hardships—I cannot cope with yours as well." That is why we must learn to be at peace in our thoughts. For, as soon as our thoughts begin to oppress us, we must turn to God and take to Him our cares and the cares of our neighbor. I always take my problems and the problems of those who come to me for advice to the Lord and His Most Holy Mother for them to resolve. And that is what they do. As for me, I cannot help even myself. How, then, can I help anyone else?

8. When our neighbor comes to us with his troubles, we take part in them, but if we do not know how to relax—to give all our infirmities and those of our neighbor to the Lord—then we bear this cumbersome burden in our own minds and hearts and, over time, we become unbearably stressed and nervous. We become irritable; we cannot stand our own selves, let alone other people around us—our family members and, of course, our co-workers. Our life becomes miserable and stressed, and our nerves become strained. This is because we have not taught ourselves to let go of our thoughts. When our thoughts are at peace, our body rests too.

9. Our plans and interests often interfere with our lives. We make all these plans, believing that we will never succeed in anything unless we arrange everything meticulously. We truly must try to do everything as our conscience tells us, but we must not do anything in haste. It is when we are in a hurry that the enemy traps us. In haste we cannot be aware of whether we have said something to offend our fellow man or whether we have ignored him, because we have no time to think of him; we are too busy with the plans inside our head. In this manner it is easy to sin against our neighbor. And when we sin against our neighbor, we are actually sinning against God, for God is everywhere. He dwells in the souls of each and every one of us. Our relationship toward our fellow men defines our relationship toward God.

It seems that we do not understand one thing: it is not good when we return the love of those who love us, yet hate those who hate us. We are not on the right path if we do this. We are the sons of light and love, the sons of God, His children. As such we must have His qualities and His attributes of love, peace, and kindness toward all.

10. Any kind of work is God's work. Every task should be performed from the heart, for it is not for people that we are laboring, but for God. God is present everywhere. The whole planet belongs to Him; the entire universe is His. No matter who your boss is, whether he is a good man who manages his company well or not, we must do our work for God. For when we work for God, our hearts and minds are open, but when we do not, we say things like, "I won't work for him; he's a lazy good-for-nothing who sits all day, yet he gets paid more than me." This is a sign that we are not performing our task from the heart. The Lord says, *Because thou art lukewarm, and neither cold nor hot, I will spew thee out of My mouth* (Rev. 3:16). We must be either hot or cold.

11. The Lord called every one of us into being with a certain goal and plan in mind. Every little blade of grass on this earth has some kind of mission here on earth, and how true this is of human beings! However, we often disturb and interfere in God's plan. We have the freedom either to accept His will or to reject it; God, Who is love, does not wish to take this freedom away from us. We have been given complete freedom, but we, in our foolishness, often have many useless desires.

12. Parents always want their children to be happy, content, and thankful to them for all their work and sacrifice. So when they see their children in a bad mood and unthankful, they're saddened. It's the same with our Heavenly Father. He has given us everything, but we are always unsatisfied and gloomy. Instead of thanking and praising God for everything, we only express our thankfulness with our lips, and our hearts remain cold. Joy is thankfulness, and when we are joyful, that is the best expression of thanks we can offer the Lord, Who delivers us from sorrow and sin.

13. The fear of God is not the animal-like fear of this world. Our fear is like that, and we must strive to conquer this. Such fear is

from hades. Our life is filled with fear. We fear what tomorrow will bring, what the future has in store for us.... That is an animal-like fear. The fear of God is when you love Him, when you truly love Him with all your heart and you strive never to offend or sadden Him—not only with your deeds, actions, and words, but also with your thoughts. You try to please Him in everything you do or say. That is the fear of God—the fear of doing anything that might sadden or offend our Parent.

14. When we are among a large number of people, say at our workplace, people often argue there, especially at large meetings. It is always best to keep silent at large gatherings. Let the others bring out their suggestions. We should keep silent. If you absolutely must say something, then say it so as not to offend anyone's dignity. It is better not to become involved. Mind your own business and try to keep your peace.

I often find that I want to defend justice, but always seem to end up having injustice done to me.... We can defend justice, but will justice be done? The Lord knows why He has permitted injustice to happen. We will not prevent injustice by our words. With words we can only offend someone and make him hurt the other person even more. We think we are defending someone, but we are, in fact, only making matters worse. If a person is in the power of the spirits of evil, such a person breeds evil. Are we going to prevent this with our words? Quite the contrary. Even if we say something while trying to defend someone from injustice, we are not doing that person a favor. The best we can do is turn to the One Who alone gives justice.

Once, at a certain gathering of Christians where there were representatives of many religious groups present, there was a Chinese man participating in one of the meetings. Every representative presented his arguments and beliefs, but the Chinese man just sat there without saying a word. When the meeting was over, they asked him, "Why didn't you give a suggestion or argue in favor or against some of the other suggestions? Why didn't you at least say something?" And he answered, "I was praying to God all the time. I was asking Him to solve the problem Himself in the best possible manner. I was praying to arrive at one decision, a decision that would benefit everyone." Now this is how one should defend justice. Not with words—words will only irritate someone and cause him to hurt others even more. We must turn to the Almighty, to Him Who is Master of all minds and hearts, and everything will be well.

The Church of the Dormition at Vitovnica Monastery, where
Elder Thaddeus lived during the latter years of his life.

CHAPTER FIVE

ON MONASTICISM

1. Our [monastic] service is a living example of sanctity and nobility. There are precious few examples of that in this life. Many are the words we hear today about how one should live, but there are very few examples. It is questionable whether we can apply all that in our lives. However, when we see a person who is peaceful and quiet, meek and humble, who does not know anger and forgives every insult, covering everything with love, such a person is a living example and we should strive to be like him. One cannot conquer evil with evil; one can only conquer evil with good.

2. We have come to this monastery from all parts. We have grown up in different families under different circumstances. Among us there are some who are too sensitive and some who are insensitive and think nothing of offending others. However, we must all tolerate one another in the community in order that we may gradually become of one mind and thought. The abbot should serve as an example to the rest of the brethren in this. If he is dissatisfied, then the whole brotherhood is dissatisfied.

3. I wish everyone, both my countrymen and all the people in the world, only good. That is what monastics are for. Once they asked me what it meant to be a monk of the great schema. The answer to this question comes from the Most Holy Theotokos herself. A monastic is one who prays for the salvation of the whole world. It is our duty to pray sincerely for all men, that God may grant peace and joy to all.

4. It is easier in a monastery. Here we are free from all the shocking things of the world. There are few connections with the outside world and that is a good thing. Of course, much depends on the person. That which is required of monks and nuns is also required of lay people. Even the Holy Fathers say that the only difference between monastics and lay people is that lay people are married. It is easier for monastics, for they do not bear the burdens of married life; they do not have to strive to raise children to be good Christians and lead them onto the right path. A monk strives for himself only. Of course, he must pray for the whole world, but it is much easier for him. But a lay person can achieve a much higher level of spirituality in meekness and humility than one who has lived as a monk in celibacy all his life, yet has not striven to achieve perfection. He who does not pray has no use for a holy place or holy things.

5. When people get married they think that everything will go smoothly, but this is not always so, for life is a battlefield. It is the same in monasteries. You go to a monastery and think that all is peaceful and quiet there, but it is not. It is a battlefield there, too.

CHAPTER SIX

ON REPENTANCE

1. We need repentance. You see, repentance is not only going to a priest and confessing. We must free ourselves from the obsession of thoughts. We fall many times during our life, and it is absolutely necessary to reveal everything [in Confession] before a priest who is a witness to our repentance.

Repentance is the renewal of life. This means we must free ourselves of all our negative traits and turn toward absolute good. No sin is unforgivable except the sin of unrepentance.

2. There are many kinds of tears. Some people cry out of rage, some to spite another person, others because they have been offended. Some cry because they have lost a loved one. There are many kinds of tears. There are also tears of repentance, when a person's conscience tells him that he has committed many sins. When he realizes his sinfulness, he weeps. That is an act of God's Grace—a soul repents, and the sin is washed away by tears. These are tears of repentance, and they are a gift from God. When a person realizes his sinfulness, he gradually frees himself from the cares of this world and from his own egoism and leaves all of his cares to the Lord. His soul is humbled, and when this occurs, it is in a state of Grace. Prayer requires a completely carefree life, for even the slightest worry disrupts our prayer, as the Holy Fathers say. Just as the slightest speck of dust can blur our vision, so, too, does the slightest worry interfere with our concentration in prayer. When we are united with the Lord, then our soul is at peace and Grace descends upon us.

A person who dwells in a state of Grace is ready to weep for anyone. He weeps when he sees the suffering of an animal, a plant, a person.... Such a person is always ready to shed tears for the whole world. That means that the Grace of God is in that person and that his tears are a gift from God. Those are tears that save. They bring a soul to perfection. Perfection cannot be reached by worrying about the things of this world. The Lord has said that we are not to burden ourselves with food and drink and with the cares of this world.

3. Often we find that those who had never previously known God have much stronger faith than those who claim to have been devout all their lives. When a person who has not known God comes to his senses and begins to pray to God, he knows what it [life] was like before and he knows Who helped him find the light at the end of the tunnel.

4. All of us sin constantly. We slip and fall. In reality, we fall into traps set by the demons. The Holy Fathers and the saints always tell us, "It is important to get up immediately after a fall and to keep on walking toward God." Even if we fall a hundred times a day, it does not matter; we must get up and go on walking toward God without looking back. What has happened has happened—it is in the past. Just keep on going, all the while asking for help from God.

5. Remembering a sin we have committed does not mean that the sin has not been forgiven. This remembrance of our sins is only a warning to us lest we become proud and sin again. In fact, we—not God—are the ones who cannot forgive ourselves. We cannot forgive ourselves because of our pride. A genuine sign that a sin has been forgiven is the fact that it has not been repeated, and we are at peace. It is also important how we spend the last years of our lives. A God-pleasing life in old age blots out the sins of youth.

6. We humans are always harvesting the fruit of our thoughts and desires. If our thoughts and desires are wicked, we cannot gather good fruit. The whole of mankind is harvesting the fruit of its thoughts and desires. The Lord said of His Second Coming, "Will I find faith?" (cf. Luke 18:8). That is why we must strive to improve our character while we are still in this life—we will pass into eternity with this very same character. We have the chance to change for the better if we repent of all our evil ways, but when a soul passes into eternity it does not have the capacity to pray for itself. I did not know this, but once I had the opportunity to feel as though my soul were about to depart my body. I felt that I could no longer pray for myself. A monk prayed for me, but I could not: my time for repentance was finished.

7. In our country and all over the world, people are reaping the fruits of their thoughts and wishes. Our desires are not good; neither are our thoughts. How then can the fruit of such thoughts and desires be good? We need to repent and change our way of life. Repentance is not just going to a priest and confessing; the soul must become free of all these thoughts and the melancholy that has overcome us due to our crooked paths. Repentance is a change of life, a change of direction, turning toward Absolute Good, and leaving behind all that is negative. True repentance is rare, even among the pious, and this is why we suffer so much. If our people were to repent, they would not experience the suffering that they are going through now. We complicate our lives terribly by our thoughts and desires. I did not know this before, but now I know that I am to blame for everything—for everything! Now I know why the Holy Fathers considered themselves to be the worst among all men.

8. When we pray for something from the depths of our heart, the Lord will grant it because He is our God and Father (cf. Matt. 7:7–11). We must strengthen ourselves in prayer and be of one

thought and one mind in our country. If we succeed in this we will not have enemies. When we look at the history of Israel we see that their enemies triumphed over them each time they fell away from the Lord, but that the Lord always helped them whenever they repented sincerely. The Lord is always with us.

CHAPTER SEVEN

ON PRAYER

1. The Lord is present everywhere. He lives in our hearts. That is why He said that we must love with all our heart and do everything willingly (cf. Matt. 22:37). When we seek the Lord from the heart, He is here! He is our Parent. Our parents in the flesh want our attention; they want us to return the love they have given us. But what happens? Very often we make them sorrowful. So when we seek God, we must do so from the heart. When we endeavor to do everything from the heart, then we have sincere, warm prayer, a love for our parents and neighbors, and the Lord is with us.

Every task we perform is at the same time a prayer. Our thoughts are focused on the job, and when we perform it from the heart, this means that we are doing it for God.[1] If we think we are doing it for anybody else, we are wrong.

Prayer from the heart is sincere prayer. Always pray to the Lord from your heart. The Lord does not require philosophy from us. We should pray from the heart, as to our Father: "O Lord, help every soul, and do not forget me, either. Help everyone to find peace and to love Thee, as the angels love Thee. Give us, too, the strength to love Thee as Thy Most Holy Mother loves Thee and Thy holy angels. Give me, too, the strength to love Thee boundlessly!"

2. The truth is that when we men pray, we read our prayer rule

---

[1] This teaching was addressed to Orthodox Christians who were living a life of accountability to God. Fr. Thaddeus was speaking about God-pleasing works.

without the participation of our entire being. We only pay lip service to our prayer rule. We are distracted, and of course that means that we are not praying in spirit and in truth (cf. John 4:23–24). We are only praying with our bodies and pronouncing the words with our lips, while our being is really somewhere else. Our attention is focused elsewhere, not on the words of the prayer. That is why the Holy Fathers say that vigilance and attention should always go before prayer. When we pray without attentiveness, then we are not praying in spirit and in truth, or in our thoughts. However, when we are attentive to what we ask for in prayer, we are concentrated on the words we speak and on that which we are asking for.

When we ask for help from someone who we know can help us, we turn to him earnestly and, with our whole being, beg him, "Please do this for me. I know you can do it." This means that we are convinced that he can help us, and so we ask him for help. But we often pray to God without attention, mechanically, and we consider that to be prayer, when actually our minds and hearts are not present. Our minds are elsewhere, or we are planning to do something and our thoughts are occupied with it, or our minds dwell on an insult.... Our minds are focused on many things except for prayer. That is why the Lord has said that God is spirit and that, when we pray, we must pray in spirit and in truth. This means that our spirit must be present when we pray.

3. The Lord is the only One who bears our burdens and cares, all our infirmities and worries, both physical and of the spirit. He can bear everything, for He is Almighty. We must give over to Him all of our infirmities and those of our neighbors, through prayer. That is what prayer is for. We must be one with the Lord and we must not worry about tomorrow, for as He says, *Sufficient unto the day is the evil thereof* (Matt. 6:34). This teaches us not to worry about tomorrow. But we do: we worry not only about tomorrow but even further than that, and this is very stressful for us. We

are rational beings, created for one day of stress at a time. Yet we torment ourselves much more than that, and therefore we suffer. We are not obedient to the Lord when He tells us not to burden our hearts with food and drink and the cares of this world. We burden our bodies and our souls. Food and drink burden the body when we eat and drink more than we need. Our bodies must work hard to digest all that food, and so they are burdened. And if we also burden ourselves with thoughts, then the stress is doubled and so is our suffering. That is why we must always be praying.

God doesn't need our prayers—we do. When we pray to God, we're actually talking to Him just as we talk to one another. God is our Father. We have no relative or friend here on earth who understands us and loves us as the Lord does. His love can't be put into words; it can be neither understood nor imagined. We're too small to understand the depth of God's love. His mercies are indescribable. He gives of Himself to us without reserve, and we can't even begin to understand this!

4. Tears flow when our thoughts are concentrated on prayer or when certain words that we read or hear touch our hearts, for example, at the Holy Liturgy. We weep when we hear words at the Holy Liturgy, Vespers, or Matins, and these words are in some way connected with our thoughts. This can also happen when we are praying alone. The Holy Fathers say that everyone, when they pray to God, can find a word that can touch their hearts, whether it be in the Psalter or in some soul-edifying book.

When all our noetic powers are concentrated in us, we can see our weaknesses clearly, and we understand that we have sinned greatly against justice, truth, and love. Then God sends purifying rain down upon us to wash us, that is, He sends us tears. That is why the Holy Fathers say that when a certain word touches our heart in that manner, we should hold on to that word for as long as possible and we should not let our attention wander anywhere else.

Not everyone is so concentrated at the Holy Liturgy so as to shed tears. Those who are free of the cares of this world and who dwell in Grace can weep at any time, anywhere. No wonder, because their thoughts and all their noetic powers are concentrated. Such a person is meek and humble and is always ready to shed tears. Whereas I, for example, who am none of these things, need a good whack on the head in order to shed a few tears, either because of pain or because of humiliation—because someone has humiliated me by striking me on the cheek. That is how I can be reduced to tears, but that is not beneficial for me, you see. But the tears that come from a humbled heart—these tears are salvific. However, tears of rage or stubbornness, or because someone has offended us, are not beneficial at all. Such tears can only harm us.

5. We cannot achieve salvation in any way other than by transforming our mind, making it different from what it was. Our minds become deified by a special act of God's Grace. They become passionless and holy. A deified mind is one which lives in remembrance of God at all times. Knowing that God is in us and we in Him, the deified mind is perfectly at home with God. He is everywhere, and we are like fish in water when we are in God. The minute our thoughts abandon Him, we perish spiritually.

6. One must prepare for Holy Communion, to become one in soul and body with our Lord, for we are His sons not only in spirit but also in body. The Lord became Man in the flesh and took upon Himself all human cares, suffering, and pain. He is the only One Who can carry this burden. He wants us to draw near to Himself with all our heart, our feelings, and our being.

7. As soon as we break the law of God, our conscience begins to bother us. It does not give us rest. And so, we must beseech the Lord in prayer that He may teach us to cleave to Him with all our heart and soul. We often forget that we are only temporary visitors

in this life and so we must abide in prayer at all times, for prayer is the breathing of our soul. Prayer draws energy from the Source of life, the Lord, Who guards, protects, and nurtures all beings.

8. No one but God knows the level of prayer that a person has attained, for if it were possible to see the amount of Grace that another has, some people would be saddened by it [because they have not reached that state].

It is detrimental for those who live in seclusion and stillness to contemplate the faces of other people and to engage in conversation with them. It is rather like hailstones falling on the tender fruit on the trees, making them wither and fall off. In the same way encounters with people, no matter how brief and for what good cause, prevent the ripening of the fruits of virtue which have flowered in silence and stillness. Just as frost burns the tender shoots of flowers that have sprung from the earth in early spring, likewise do encounters with people burn the fruit of the mind that has begun to sprout virtue.

9. There are very few people who come to their senses, very few who understand life. We pray with our lips only, and we hurry through our prayers to "get it over with" as soon as possible, and then we lose peace. Fasting and prayer are a means of embellishing our soul and bringing it back to its original state. We must strive, with God's help, to attain the traits of Christ the Savior. We know that He was meek, humble, and good, and we must try to imitate Him. However, we have no strength to do this by ourselves; therefore we must ask the Lord for help. It is impossible for the light bulb to give us light without electrical power, and it is impossible for us to live without God; as He Himself said, *Without Me you can do nothing* (John 15:5).

10. They taught me how to pray the Jesus Prayer [at Miljkovo Monastery]. I prayed all the time, and it often happened that

although I might have been engaged in conversation with another person, I still heard the words of the Jesus Prayer which came from my heart on their own. I felt indescribable joy, and there was nothing that could make me angry. Thoughts about the things of this world had no place in my heart as I was in a state of Grace. Let us remember the state that the Most Holy Mother of God was in. She lived in the Grace of the Holy Spirit all her life.

I have always loved music, even from my earliest childhood. But when I was in that state of Grace and tried to recall a certain melody, it would not come to mind. The prayer flowed quietly and joyfully, and I could not remember any tunes. However, as soon as one's attention turns to the things of this world, one's zeal ebbs away.

11. When we see a certain object, we very often want to possess it, but once we do, we quickly lose interest in it. As soon as we see something else we long after it, and so it goes on endlessly. We are extremely volatile. This is why the Lord came to dwell among us men, to gather and unite us together so that we may be one flock under one Shepherd. When He embraces us everything is easy. Now our thoughts are distracted. They are not focused on what we are doing. The only remedy for this is prayer. Any task requires a concentration of the mind, most especially prayer.

The Holy Fathers speak of noetic prayer, the Jesus Prayer. There is a series of rules on how to employ the Jesus Prayer and how to let one's mind descend into the heart, but it is necessary to have an experienced spiritual guide in order for one to learn the Jesus Prayer in the right way.

12. Prayer is something that must be practiced always. Every movement of the heart must be prayerful. The Holy Fathers say that just as even the smallest speck of dust prevents us from seeing, so too does even the slightest care prevent us from praying. A carefree life is needed for pure prayer.

13. The Most Holy Mother of God has appeared and spoken to many people in recent times. She has said that she prays to her Son for us, but that there is no repentance among us. She has instructed us on many occasions to repent, because time is accelerating and hard days are ahead for Christians. She tells us that we will have to repent so as not to share the fate of those who have fallen away from God.

The Holy Fathers say that the earth offered the cave in which the Savior was born, and mankind gave Him the Most Holy Mother of God.[1] This was so that the Lord could descend among us and become man in order to save us. He took on our nature in order to transform and renew it. And all who are in the Lord Jesus Christ are a new creation, new men.

Life on earth is too brief, so brief that we cannot even imagine. But much has been provided for us in this brief period of time that we are in this life. It has been given to us so that we can always turn to God from the depth of our heart. He is the One Who can transform and resurrect our souls. Christians are very, very fortunate indeed to have the Most Holy Mother of God interceding for them before the throne of God.

You can also see that here, in this life, when we ask our parents for something, they will grant it—if we are obedient to them, of course. The Most Holy Mother of God prays without ceasing to her Son for us.

14. The Lord is not tired of hearing us complain all the time. He is tired of our sins, not our turning to Him for help. He wants us to call upon Him all the time and to pour out our hearts to Him. Prayer should not be something that is said and forgotten. You stand in front of an icon, recite your prayers, and go about your business. That is not prayer.

---

[1] See Vespers for the Nativity of Christ, fourth sticheron (in the Festal Menaion).

15. Strong faith in a man's heart both requires and produces prayer, and a prayer life of many years produces love. The goal of our life is nothing other than cleansing our heart to such an extent that it is able to sing with joy. Thus, prayer of the heart leads to joy of the heart. Nothing is difficult for a joyful person, because he has love.

16. The Holy Fathers have written much about noetic prayer and on how to control one's mind and heart. They have said that we must endeavor to perform every task, every kind of work, from the heart, because feelings come from the heart, not from the head. We think with the head, but when everything proceeds from the heart, this is a concentration of all the powers of the mind in the heart. When we pray, we must do so from the heart, for God is the Lord of the heart. He is the center of the life of every living being. He is the moving Power of life, and we ought not look for Him anywhere else. He is here, waiting for us to accept Him and to put our trust in Him.

17. A young man from Bosnia used to come to me here. He lived in the world and prayed the Jesus Prayer. This young man had a friend who was married and had children and a job. This friend was not particularly pious at the time, but he was a good man. One day the young man mentioned the Jesus Prayer to his friend. "Why don't you try praying the Jesus Prayer," he said. "I can teach you how." So he taught him and gave him a prayer rope.[1] In a very short time his friend received the gift of Grace, and both he and his family were transformed. The first young man had been practicing the Jesus Prayer for so long, yet he did not receive the gift of Grace.

After a while, the other young man came to see me and said, "Father, it is as though I have been enlightened by a special kind of joy and a peace I cannot describe. In my heart I constantly hear

---

[1] *Prayer rope:* a looped rope with knots, used for saying the Jesus Prayer or other similar short prayers.

the words, "Lord Jesus Christ, Son of God, have mercy on me, a sinner." I know what I was like before, the kind of thoughts that I had, but now there is nothing like that in my mind anymore. I used to have lustful thoughts for the opposite sex; I used to get angry for the slightest reason, but now—I cannot explain how—I just cannot get angry. I do not know what has happened to me. No bad thoughts come to me now, even if I want them to.... The only feeling that is left in me now is joy—an ineffable joy has taken over my entire being." I told him that he had been given the gift of Grace and that he would have it for as long as he could keep his thoughts away from the cares of this world. If he were to do that [i.e., return his thought to the cares of the world], I told him, he would stop hearing the words of the Jesus Prayer in his heart, and then the joy and peace would gradually disappear from his heart. He would again become laden with the cumbersome thoughts generated by the prince of this world. I told him that if he wished to keep the gift of Grace he had been given, he was to pray to God ceaselessly in order to block the thoughts that come from the realm of the demons and thus preserve the joy and peace that he was feeling.

18. One should pray as Fr. John of Kronstadt did: he read the prayers with attentiveness and when he felt his heart warming to a certain word, his soul would be filled with joy and peace and he would continue to pray with feeling.

We should say the words of the prayers knowing that the Lord sees us and that He is listening to us. When something "moves" in the heart while we are at prayer, we should hold on to it and try to preserve that feeling.

19. We have been called to pray, keep vigil, and do good, but if we do not strive to become like Christ, then all is in vain.

20. A vigilant heart is needed for a spiritual life. Such a heart is

always burning with love. When the period of warfare comes, we are overwhelmed by thoughts and cares of all sorts. This is when we must turn to the Lord in our hearts and keep silence. If we cannot abandon the thought that is bothering us immediately, then we must keep silence. We should not think about anything. It is not ours to think. The Lord knows what we can take and what we cannot. Then, when we are in silence and our mind is quiet, we should give it something to do so that it will not wander. We should pray. Let the mind pray from the heart. Thus, gradually, we will become accustomed to prayer, and prayer will become a habit to us, just like any task that we learn to perform. Pray in this manner, without words, and when the Lord sees our endeavors, when He sees that we seek Him and wish to be with Him in all eternity, then He will give us strength, and the heart then will dwell in constant prayer. Then we will do our work while listening to the prayer in us.

21. We know that the Lord became man, and we know Him as a Man. He came that near to us. He came close to us, not only in spirit, but also in the flesh, for we are His kin. Since this is so, we must strive to get close to Him in our heart. When we think about a certain person often, we begin to love that person. Do you understand? It is impossible to love a person if we do not pay any attention to him for a long time and do not think about him.

Let us think about the Lord in the same way, all the time. We know that all strength comes from Him—why should we ever ask anybody else to help us? Who is more mighty than He? We must seek Him in our hearts, for that is where He is. He is never far away. He is the center of life and its moving force.

When we seek the Lord, our heart begins to burn. The heart is warmed, and if our thoughts are concentrated in one point and the concentration is powerful, then the flame of the heart grows stronger and stronger, and we do everything from the heart. After that we see things around us changing—people's thoughts also start to change—all because of the peace that radiates from us. We see the thoughts of people around us actually changing! The people are changing! They feel good in our presence. Perhaps they had been at war with us before, but now they feel us radiating peace. As for us, we now no longer return "an eye for an eye," but rather good and kind thoughts. We are no longer at war with them; we have stopped the warfare. What we want is peace. When there are two warring sides, one side has to back down for the sake of peace. We are that side. The Lord has, after all, commanded us to love our enemies.

22. When you are praying, you must pay close attention to the words of the prayer you are reading. That is where your attention must be at all times. The mind is capable of coming up with all sorts of images. We can conjure up anything in our thoughts. In such a state we may think we are having a vision and may be totally convinced that what we are seeing is true. We must not do that. Our minds are very distracted. The Holy Fathers say that there are only four things we may think about during prayer. We are not exactly to think of them but to bear them in mind. These are death, the Judgment, heaven, and hell.

Everyone should remember his own death and bear in mind the end of his life, or at least be aware that this life is very, very short. Life goes by very quickly and old age comes suddenly. See, it is as though World War II happened yesterday, when in fact forty years have gone by. Forty years, almost the lifespan of a person! And so, we must know that being aware of the briefness of life is our awareness of death. This is what we should think about.

We will have to give an answer for the kind of life we have led. We will give an answer as to how we used the energy that was given us. This energy is Divine energy and Divine strength.... We will have to answer for how we have helped in this life. Have we helped by disseminating peace and harmony in the universe, or have we contributed to the existing chaos? For this reason we must always strive to perfect our thoughts.

Death, the Judgment, heaven, and hell. We must have a remembrance of these things all the time. As for our attention, it must be focused on the words of the prayer.

The Lord only appears to us when the need is great. We are too weak to be able to recognize a vision from the other world and we have no discernment. This is very dangerous for the soul. The Holy Fathers have often prayed never to have any visions. When the soul is unable to find comfort anywhere in the world, then the Lord Himself comes to comfort it. This only happens in extreme necessity.

23. QUESTION: Father, I am trying to make my mind descend into my heart by controlling my breathing, as the Holy Fathers teach, but I feel as though there is no place in my heart, I feel something like a light pressure and a slight discomfort. What should I do?

ANSWER: This is because your mind has not descended into your heart at all, but has produced thoughts on its own. This is dangerous and there is the possibility of losing one's mind. It sometimes happens to students as well, when there is too much stress on the blood vessels in their brain. You should not attempt to do this without an experienced spiritual guide who will explain to you how to let your mind down into your heart. It is difficult to find such a spiritual guide today. What you can do is understand that every task you do is done for God. When you have realized and accepted that, then you no longer need to think about letting your mind descend into your heart.

You think that your mind is in your heart, but your mind is still where it was before, in your head. Many have practiced the Jesus Prayer by themselves but have lost their minds.

CHAPTER EIGHT

ON LOVE

1. God is Love. And if we call upon God in our life as the Holy Fathers teach us, then we are calling upon Love. If we know and believe that He is present everywhere at all times and if we are united with Him in our hearts, He will teach us how to love our neighbor. For we do not know how to love either the Lord or our neighbor. The evil spirits often so interfere with the Divine love given us by God that they often lure us away from the path of real and true love. Their suggestions are full of the physical and emotional aspects of this world: enjoyment and lust, which is nothing but enslavement.

It often happens that a person, either young or old, falls in love with another person or even an object. Some people fall in love with gold and cannot bear to be separated from it or from their wealth, house, and possessions, and they become enslaved. If someone were to take this from them, they would become desperate. Many times the powers of evil bring such people to the brink of self-destruction.

Is this love? The spirits of evil often come and meddle with the Divine love that God has planted in us. That kind of love [corrupted by the evil spirits] is without discernment. But the love of God is boundless.... Love is perfection, says the Apostle (cf. Rom. 13:10). God is perfect, He is faultless. And so, when Divine love becomes manifest in us in the fullness of Grace, we radiate this love not only on the earth, but throughout the entire universe as well. So God is in us, and He is present everywhere. It is God's all-encompassing love that manifests itself in us. When this happens we see no difference between people—everyone is good, everyone is our brother, and we consider ourselves to be the worst of men, servants of every created thing.

In this kind of love we are humbled; our soul is at peace and in humility. And humility is the perfection of the Christian life. It is not in the raising of the dead or in working miracles that Christian perfection lies, but in extreme humility. When we are illumined by the Grace of the Holy Spirit in the fullness of Divine love, then we want to serve everyone and help everyone. Even when we see a little ant struggling, we want to help him.

So, love is sacrifice. Love sacrifices itself for its neighbor.

2. The Lord is always waiting for us to unite ourselves with Him in love, but instead we drift further and further away from Him. We know that there can be no life without love. This means that there is no life without God, for God is Love. But His love is not according to the understanding of this world. The love that the world gives us consists of suffering and enslavement because the spirits of evil interfere with it. There is a little bit of love, but mostly it is just enslavement. The spirits of evil try to enslave us so that we become tied to certain people or things, in order to prevent our hearts from going out to God, the Source of life and love. For they know that if our hearts unite with Him, then they cannot come close to us. The man who is given Grace and who is united with God's love is also protected by this Divine love, and the evil spirits cannot come close to him.

3. Love is the most powerful means of defense there is. There are no weapons and no power that can measure themselves against love. Everything is defeated before love.

4. All of nature is a great mystery, from the plants and birds to man, for God is present everywhere. He discloses a small part of this great mystery to those who truly love Him—to men of

pure heart. God is an incomprehensible energy. Man also has incomprehensible energy. When these two energies are in harmony, we have paradise on earth, joy, and all-encompassing love.

5. We can all be good if, with all our hearts, we unite ourselves with the Source of life, God. He will give us strength to love both ourselves and our neighbor. Without God it is not possible to love oneself, even. Many people become depressed and hopeless and attempt to take their own lives, for without God we cannot even love ourselves, let alone our friends, family, and neighbors—or our enemies for that matter. All is possible with God, for He is our strength and our life. We must give our heart to someone, and if we give it to any person on this planet, this person can harm us. We all seek boundless and unchangeable love and infinite peace, but who can give it to us? Not even our parents, our brothers, or our sisters. Every one of them can abandon, despise, or harm us. Why? Because we are all limited by time and space and we all battle against the unclean powers, which are constantly defiling our thoughts.

6. To whomever we give our heart, this person can harm us or abandon us. The spirits of wickedness are constantly putting evil thoughts into our feeling of love and preying on us. Divine love is boundless and all-encompassing, whereas we are attached to men and the lifeless things of this world. Our hearts have been imprisoned by the things of this world, and if those things are taken away from us, our hearts are saddened and they suffer.

One must love God first, and only then can one love one's closest of kin and neighbors. We must not be as idols to one another, for such is not the will of God.

Elder Thaddeus.

CHAPTER NINE

ON THE FALLEN WORLD

1. We who are fallen, like the fallen spirits, allow ourselves to become enslaved by things or people. Not so the angelic hosts. And those among us who unite themselves to the Lord in their hearts and minds never become slaves to any created thing. They are with the Lord and together with Him they love all of creation. It is quite unbelievable—in such a state one feels that all men, good or bad, are one's kin. The only thing which makes us sad is that their thoughts oppose love and goodness.

2. All that God created, He created as sublime and perfect. Even the spirits that later fell away from God were created as perfect beings. They fell away from noetic perfection, and because they have alienated themselves from the Source of life, they seek solace in a life of falsehood. They have no real life but seek it amid created things, amid things that are limited. That is the food they thrive on. But because they have alienated themselves from love—yet remember how it was when they were under the wing of the Holy Spirit in the fullness of Grace—they try to imitate that [love], and thus entice people, giving them false comfort in order to win them over.

And so people engage in many activities: philosophy, rational thinking, scientific research—but all that is very short-lived. The comfort lasts a very short time, and then depression and despondency set in. People on this earth generally feel very lonely, even when they are among their closest family members. This is due to our fallen nature. The children cry, and their cries are also the cries of their parents.

The fallen spirits also feel loneliness and therefore keep company with each other, doing all kinds of evil, just like the people here on the earth. The fallen spirits are of one mind and they act together, whatever they do, trying to find consolation, but they never find it. Likewise people: they go to bars and restaurants together and get drunk, smashing glasses and bottles, and they come home with cuts and bruises, but they find no comfort. They look for comfort everywhere, but it cannot be found. But those who are one with the Lord, like the angels, are always at peace and have joy in their hearts. Their peace and joy are unchangeable.

3. It is just as the Holy Fathers say: The spirits that have fallen from the heights of perfection are now on the earth, and they can see that their time is running out. The time is approaching when the era from the creation of the world to the Dread Judgment will finally be over. The fallen spirits suffer greatly, for they know that there will be a Judgment and that it will be just. They know that after the Judgment they will be isolated. Right now they have a certain freedom. They move among people, creating delusions and winning many people over to their side. They believe that victory will be theirs, but, in the end, Divine justice will prevail.

4. We are very peculiar beings, we humans. We have been given wonderful things by the Lord, yet we do not seem to realize that this is so. We have fallen, and because of the Fall of man, all of creation suffers, for man was created to be the master of the material world.

The material world was created as sublime, not coarse and rough as it is today. After Adam transgressed the Lord's commandment, everything became coarse. This is why the Apostle Paul says, *The whole creation groaneth* and *waiteth for the manifestation of the sons of God* (Rom. 8:22, 19). Nature is waiting for us to be delivered in order that it, too, might be delivered from corruption, for in its present state it is corrupt and changeable. And in us, in our bodies, there exist all the substances and the minerals that can be found in the universe. Once we were the masters of all material things, but now everything is rebelling against us, for we are to be blamed for the fall of all things. We must become better in order for everything to be renewed.

5. The older generations still remember how we Serbs used to be before the war [World War II], compared to what we are like now. Before the war there were also dances in all the towns and villages, and the young people would gather together to dance and sing. But these dances began in the afternoon, after lunch, and as soon as the sun began to set everyone went home. Today our young people go out at ten or eleven at night and have turned day into night. What good can we expect?

6. Just as the body dies when the soul leaves it, so too does the soul die when the Holy Spirit abandons it.[1] Death is a result of sin because both death and corruption are the fruit of sin in the soul, and it is through sin that the soul dies to eternal life and becomes separated from the Holy Spirit and the Kingdom of God. But the soul that has become one with God is meek and humble, always in prayer and always standing in the presence of God. Such a soul never permits itself to become distracted.

---

[1] St. Gregory Palamas explains what is meant by the death of the soul: "Physical death is when the soul leaves the body and is separated from it. The death of the soul is when God leaves the soul and is separated from it, although in another way, the soul remains immortal. Once separated from God it becomes more ugly and useless than a dead body, but unlike such a body it does not disintegrate after death since it is not composite" (St. Gregory Palamas, *Homilies* [Waymart, Pa.: Mount Thabor Publishing, 2009], p. 118).

7. Mankind used to be united, but sin has produced a rift between us and now we have no unity. It is because of this that the Lord came—to bring together that which has been divided by sin. The angels in the Kingdom of God are of one mind and one thought, they abide in harmony, but we men, we are divided.

We live in families with our parents, brothers, and sisters and yet we are unsatisfied, we feel lonely and each one of us is burdened with his own cares. We want to leave our families and be with someone else; we long to cleave to that other person and spend our lives with him or her. God, when He created Adam, said that it is not good for man to be alone, and so He created a companion for him. Adam and Eve were one in the eyes of God.

But everything went wrong after the Fall. The Lord said, *Be fruitful, and multiply, and replenish the earth* (Gen. 1:28). We do not know how reproduction would have taken place if man had not fallen. The earth was to have been filled with people.[1]

At that time our forefathers did not have the corruptible and mortal bodies that we have. After the Fall, God Himself had to come down to the fallen world, to transfigure and resurrect it and bring it back to its original state. When the day of the Final Judgment comes, we will once more receive incorruptible bodies, which will also be spiritual bodies.

After the Fall, nothing was as it had been before, not even physical matter. The Lord wanted to transfigure, with His coming, not only mankind but also the entire material world. The Holy Apostle Paul says that everything that exists in the universe will be brought back into its original state of incorruption (cf. Rom. 8:20–21). On the Day of Judgment, the Lord will remove all the

---

[1] According to Sts. Athanasius the Great (*Commentary on the Psalms* [Psalm 50:5]), Gregory of Nyssa (*On the Making of Man* 17), John Chrysostom (*On Virginity* 14–15), Maximus the Confessor (*Ambiguum* 41), John Damascene (*Exact Exposition of the Orthodox Faith* 4.24), and Symeon of Thessaloniki (*On the Sacraments* 38), if man had not fallen, God would have employed a means of increasing the human race other than sexual reproduction.

elements from the material world; He will remove them at a speed greater than the speed of light. He will say the word and it will happen. And all that was will pass away, and a new heaven and a new earth will appear in the place of the old (cf. II Pet. 3:13; Rev. 21:1). There will be no more time, and instead of the sun, the Lord will shine (cf. Rev. 10:6, 21:23).

What joy there will be and what a revelation it will be, even for the angels! The Apostle said that even the angels wish to peer into the mystery of the Holy Church, into its depths (cf. I Pet. 1:12).

Oh, how unthankful we are, and how much we have cleaved to the corrupt things of this world!

8. We are too engrossed in things of this world and thus become spiritually impoverished, because one cannot sit on two chairs. One cannot drink both from the Cup of the Savior and from the cup of the adversary. We must decide whom we will serve: God or the things of this world. One cannot serve God and mammon at the same time.

9. The Lord wants to make us clean and to give us of His Divine power and strength. But we are not pure or cleansed of evil. Were He to give us His powers in our impure state, they would turn to black magic.

10. Because God is present everywhere, the fallen spirits cannot do what they want. They can harm us mostly through other people. We can protect ourselves from them only with the power of God. Man has been given great strength, and if we could only concentrate our thoughts in prayer, the fallen spirits would not be able to harm us or to do anything contrary to the will of God. Where there is prayer, the fallen spirits have no power.

11. We make it very hard for God to appear to us when we are like a broken mirror in which even spiritual themes reflect and

refract in the fragments in a hundred different ways. We all receive only as much as we can take and always in proportion to the "broken mirror" with which we come into the world. Christ came into the world in order to make our mirror whole again, so that we can receive God's image in it. Of course, there are many who cannot conceive of the idea of God or accept Him into their hearts.

Our bodies, in the state they are in now, would not be able to stand the intensity of the light of God. This is a possible reason why many saints, having been illumined by the light of God after a long and victorious struggle against all manner of temptations, passed into eternity shortly after receiving the light. Their joy is great in the Kingdom of God, for they are one with God and other pious souls who glorify Him.

The mind, heart, and will are usually divided and separated in the ordinary person. This is the most common source of our problems and afflictions. However, with those who have been enlightened by God, the mind, heart, and will are united, and the light they have been given is not only the visible, physical light that they radiate, but a much deeper and permanent inner light whose abode is the person's heart. This light is love, and it is only with love that man can draw near to God, Who is pure Love. Our growth and journey toward God is eternal, for God is indescribable, ineffable, and uncontainable. However, it is through love that we are closest to Him.

12. Our wishes and goals in this life will not be irrelevant. A spiritual person has struggled to attain the Kingdom of Heaven, and a person of this world has fought for the things of this world. At first sight it may seem that there is only a very slight difference between a person who believed in the idea of earthly justice and perhaps even gave his life for the fulfillment of this idea, and a person who believed in the idea of heavenly justice which is never fulfilled in this world. However, the difference is huge. And so, in

spite of the ostensible faith, honor, and sacrifice of a person who struggles for justice in the world, this person's desires continue to develop in the wrong direction even after death, and he will find himself with the wrong people! Kindred souls seek each other out both here and there.

13. We criticize our politicians who are currently in power but they, too, are our children. It is we, the older generation, who are to blame, for we have not set a good example for them. We are an image of our parents, of the former older generation, and from them we were not able to learn much. Now we are to blame, because we have failed to lead our children onto the right path. We must begin with ourselves and not try to change others. The Holy Fathers say that we must correct ourselves—to work on our salvation and many around us will be saved. We must strive to always be kind, good, and quiet—at peace so that people will always feel peace and quietness in our presence. We know that we can either attract people with our thoughts or drive them away from us. We need to change so that our faith might be strengthened.

14. The Holy Fathers say that the Lord has permitted mankind to be born of woman and to multiply on the earth in this manner because of the Fall of our forebears. God had ordered everything perfectly, and He is the Father of all. However, after the Fall this harmony was disturbed. Our very nature became corrupt, for our forebears were created immortal. When man fell, death came and the order of the universe was disturbed, for Adam had been created as the crown of the universe and the master of all created things. In every man can be found the entire material world of the universe and all the noetic powers. This is why it has been said that man is a microcosm. We must return to the bosom of our Heavenly Father and our faith must grow stronger in order that we might get strength from Him, and we shall see His Kingdom.

15. After the Fall everything fell apart. God, being Love, knew that created beings would not be able to remain in the state they were created in, and so He gave them all the time from the Creation to the Dread Judgment to come to their senses and return to the bosom of their Heavenly Father, to become one with Absolute Good and Absolute Love.

Mankind, however, prefers evil to good. Such is the result of our fallen nature! It is easier for us to think evil than good. But when we think evil, we have no peace or rest from such thoughts. How great is our fall! It is a strange thing indeed.... We cannot seem to come to our senses, neither can we do good of our own selves. We have no idea how very much our thoughts are tyrannized by the fallen spirits. We think those are our thoughts. We are tormented by hatred, envy, and malice. Unsurpassed tyranny! Our soul does not want this, but it cannot free itself. It becomes accustomed to this tyranny from a very early age, so that it has become rooted firmly in the soul. One must strive to conquer this tyranny of thoughts! We must be transformed into love and acquire peace. It is not easy, for our fall is very great!

Man cannot do this without God's help. Man thinks very highly of himself. But everything that is revealed to him comes from eternity. We are surrounded by God's mysteries. We ourselves are the greatest mystery. We don't even know who we are, where we came from, and where we are going. What sort of a being is this that thinks, moves, and talks without knowing how or why? What a great mystery this is! How is it possible that our internal organs function without our will—and they function perfectly at that? And how is it that we can disturb this perfect harmony with our thoughts?

16. What is a life? Nothing! It is difficult to comprehend how short life is. A young person does not understand this.

It has occurred to me many times that we are miserable wretches indeed, we who live on the earth: we cannot live even so long as four billion seconds, which is 120 years. One hundred years is three billion seconds. What is a hundred years? Nothing! A moment.... Our life is in eternity.

17. As for people, they are never satisfied. Nothing is enough. This began right after the fall of our forebears, when Cain slew Abel out of envy, because Abel's sacrifice was pleasing to God and Cain's wasn't. That is when it all started. Today there is no peace. Everyone behaves as though they will live forever. It really seems as though the end is very near. The factories pollute the environment so much that very soon life will not be possible.

Animals have the joy of living, but we have taken it away from them. They have joy, and we have so much besides joy, yet we are never satisfied. The animals never worry about the future, they do not stack food in granaries and barns, yet the Lord always feeds them. They nibble a twig here, peck at a seed there, they find protection in a hole or a burrow, and they are grateful to God. Not so us men. The birds are always singing praises to the Lord. They begin their song early, at three o'clock in the morning, and don't stop until nine. At nine they calm down a little bit—it's only then that they go looking for food to feed their young. Then they start singing again. Nobody tells them to sing—they just do. And what about us? We're always frowning, always pouting; we don't feel like singing or doing anything else. We should follow the example of the birds. They're always joyful whereas we're always bothered by something. What is it that bothers us? Nothing, really.... Isn't that right?

18. Life on earth is not easy, no matter how favorable the circumstances. There is one person who lived according to his heart's desire, and that was King Solomon, the son of King David. He ruled for forty years and never went to war. The Lord rewarded him with great wisdom. He built the great temple of Jerusalem. People came to him from all over the world in order to hear his

advice. He said, "I have fulfilled every desire of my heart. I wished for vineyards and I planted them. I wished for palaces and I built them. In Jerusalem I had the best trained army, but I never went to war with anyone. I wished for silver and gold, and the Lord gave them to me. I engaged in different things in order to see whether there was any lasting comfort on earth. And I understood that in this life everything is vanity and pride and sickness of spirit. There is no lasting comfort...." These are Solomon's words. Solomon was wise. He says that whatever you may possess will be for a brief time only, and then it will be as though you had never existed. A man thinks that he has all the wisdom of this world. But if he could look at himself as others see him, he would see himself strutting like a turkey. He would see his own vanity and empty-headedness....

Is there anyone on this earth who knows everything? No. Each one of us is perfected in a certain area of knowledge, and that is how we form a whole. People are very respectful of philosophers and scientists; they are always quoting their words. No one seems to remember that God promised our forefathers that He would send the Savior of mankind, Who would bring us back to our original state. They did not know that God Himself would become incarnate on earth. For only the One Who has created us can bring us back to our original state. And He came, and men did not receive Him.

CHAPTER TEN

ON SPIRITUAL STRUGGLE

1. Everything is constantly changing; nothing remains static. We perfect ourselves either in good or in evil.

2. We must learn how to live a heavenly life. And that is not easy, because up until now we have led a life of resistance and opposition. Take, for example, a family man who has a home and a family and who knows how to do his job well but is doing this job against his will. That is how inner resistance builds up. If we do not learn to rid ourselves of this inner resistance, we will not be able to enter the Kingdom of Heaven and dwell among the angels and the saints. For we have acquired the habit of always opposing one thing or another, as there is always something that is against our will. We have not learned to be obedient to the will of God but always want our will to be done. Well, in that case there will be no place for us in heaven.

Therefore, let us be thankful to God for everything. He knows why He has put us in the position where we find ourselves, and we will get the most out of it when we learn to be humble.

We should always remember that whatever task we perform here in this life is for Him. He gives it to us; whether we are believers or not, whether we are pious or not, we must carry out God's plan.

3. The evil spirits are always wanting to interfere with whatever we are doing for our salvation. Alas, we who are lukewarm usually say to ourselves, "Wait, I have not yet done this, I have not yet

tried that ... I will repent later. After I have done all these things I will repent, God, and I will walk the straight path, wandering neither to the right nor to the left." This is exactly what the spirits of evil want us to do; they want us to put off our salvation until tomorrow, or the day after, and so on and so forth, until the end of our life. But the Holy Fathers say, "Go with the Lord, go today, follow Him!"

4. May the Lord give us Serbs and the whole world the spiritual strength to transform ourselves. We know that time is running out, and the evil spirits know this, too. They do not want a single person to be free from evil thoughts. With that aim, they teach even small children to oppose their parents so that, when these children grow up, they will be easy prey for them. One can see what the spirits of evil are doing with our youth: these young people offend their parents and other adults, and they have no peace.

But it can all take a turn for the good if each one of us begins with himself, if the transformation starts with us. We should try to have good thoughts which will radiate from us. A meek and humble person is always very pleasant to be with, for he emanates peace and warmth. That person may not say a single word, yet we rejoice to be in his presence. So, if we all begin with ourselves, transformation will take place. Goodness will be renewed and established all around us, in our country and further abroad.

I have often listened to stories of the older people about how we Serbs used to be before the Wars of Liberation in 1912. All the older people had prayer ropes and prayed to God. After 1912 things began to deteriorate, and after World War I everything took a turn for the worse. Those who are old enough to remember life between World Wars I and II know that the difference between then and now is huge. To me, this world looks as though it has just come out of hades!

5. We are very peculiar beings, and we often wonder at all the mysteries that surround us. We know a little bit about the world, but this is really very little.

In the first place, we are a mystery to our own selves. Who are we and what are we? we wonder. No one asked us to be born, and no one will ask us when we will depart this life. Our life span is very brief, but even during this brief time we have been given many opportunities to perfect ourselves in good and to turn toward the Absolute Good. Only when we do so will our horizons expand and some answers become clearer to us, such as why the world exists and why it is the way it is. We will understand that it is because of us, that we are to blame for the state of the world today. We will realize that we are constantly destroying peace, love, and joy. Yet, when we become united with the Source of life, everything will become clear. We Christians have been called to spread Divine peace and the atmosphere of heaven. There are very few of those who realize that this is how we should be—a source of goodness, peace, and joy.

6. The seal of the Holy Spirit is in our heart, which bears the fruits of our life. Meekness, peace, a merciful heart, goodness, kindness, faith, and abstinence are some of the fruits of tears offered to Christ from the heart. The results of such tears are love of one's enemies and prayers offered up to the Lord for them. Tears give us strength to be joyful even in times of great suffering and tribulation and to look upon the sins of others as our own and repent for them. Tears make it possible for us to lay down our life for our brother.

7. The Holy Fathers have taught us how to fast. Those who are physically weak and sick do not need to fast; they can take Holy Communion without fasting. But we who are physically healthy must prepare for Communion by fasting. This means that we eat less and only certain kinds of food, for by doing so we discipline

our bodies and our thoughts. When the body is humbled, our thoughts become more peaceful, too. This is the purpose of fasting. God is present in a mysterious way in every being, most especially in the heart, which is the center of life. It is impossible to unite with God when the stomach is full, for a full stomach causes many cares and worries. All our thoughts, all our emotions, and all our will must be concentrated. When they are not, we are restless and lose our peace.

8. The Lord endowed all of us with free will. He knows all things because, for Him, time is irrelevant. For God, all eternity is today, the present moment. This is impossible for us to understand, but that is because we are limited. Every human being who comes into this world is unique, and all are given the opportunity to know God. Since we have the gift of free will, we often abuse it. For example, there are people who eat in moderation and others who eat more than their bodies need. Those who are moderate usually live longer and are healthier. It is the same in the spiritual life. Some people have quiet and peaceful thoughts, whereas others are not satisfied with that, so they go overboard and sometimes must run into a wall in order to go back to the straight path!

9. The Lord knows all things; He knew us even before we were conceived. That is why He gave us the law of obedience through Moses on Mount Sinai. This law was given because of us who need correction, not because of the meek and humble ones. They do not need this law. The law of obedience is necessary for the correction of our will and to set our free will on the path of humility, righteousness, and love. Obedience is necessary for maintaining harmony.

The angels are completely obedient, and their harmony and love are perfect. We too must imitate their model of obedience in our relationship with our parents. The Holy Fathers say that obedience is greater even than fasting or prayer. This is something

I did not understand very well when I was younger. If we have no obedience, then our fasting is in vain.

We know that every good gift comes from the Holy Spirit. The Holy Fathers made themselves worthy of receiving these gifts through prayer and fasting, but above all they had obedience.

10. We must learn to bow down before the will of God and not insist on our will. Obedience to the will of God is carried out through obedience to our elders, parents, teachers, supervisors at work.... If we have obedience we will understand what is required of us.

11. Our life on this earth is such that we are always becoming enslaved to material things, while the angels never are. This life was given to us so that we may learn about eternal life, that we may learn how to become free, to walk freely and with a clear conscience and pure thoughts. When we are free, then there are no spiritual battles or warfare; victory is ours only because we have abandoned ourselves to God, because we worship Him in our hearts and have united with Him, giving no more thought to this world. He is the One Who determines our life, and we receive everything that comes to us as from His own hand.

12. He who does not sacrifice himself like a lamb led to slaughter for even the least virtue and who does not shed blood in order to attain virtue—such a person will never attain virtue. God, by His Divine providence, has established it so: we attain eternal life by our voluntary death. If you will not die a voluntary death, you cannot attain eternal life and you will be dead. He who does not die a perfect death by cutting off his own will, shall not enter the Kingdom of Heaven.

If you have been worthy of being a God-bearer, watch lest you do anything unworthy of His holy will. Otherwise He will depart from you, and you will lose the treasure that is in you.

Respect Him in all things to the best of your ability, and never accept into His dwelling anything that is contrary to His will, lest you anger Him and He depart from you. Never speak or pray without a totally pious concentration of your thoughts. Never think, "Let me show Him warmth and zealous love so that He will know how much I love and respect Him," for He knows your thoughts even before you have conceived them. There is nothing hidden from Him.

If you dare keep Him by force, you will immediately feel an emptiness inside, for He is uncontainable. He will distance Himself, and even if you become contrite and repent with tears, you will not benefit from your tears. This is true, for He is Joy and will not enter a dwelling that is full of gloom and sadness, just as a hard-working bee will not enter a place that is full of smoke. But if you become carefree and give yourself over to His will, He will come and dwell in you again.

Never say to yourself, "If I do not pray with tears, He will depart from me as from an indolent man." If God had wanted you to attain perfection by weeping, He would have watched you from afar and would have concealed Himself completely from you. He would have encouraged your tears for the cleansing of the dwelling of your heart. But now, after your repentance and the cleansing you have received from Him, He has come to you in order to give you rest and to fill you with joy and peace in place of sadness.

Stand upright, not with your body but with the movements and inclination of your soul. Establish stillness and continuous prayer and prepare the home of your soul for the King of kings to enter. Command all your servants (that is, your feelings and emotions): "The King is coming, stand upright at the doors, stand with peace and fear." Watch, lest thieves knock on the doors; do not permit any voice, from within or without, to enter the chamber of the King. Watch, lest someone deceive you and come inside, for then the King will depart from your dwelling.

Be joyful and filled with exultation, yet also be watchful and listen to what He will be pleased to tell you. He has no need of any services performed by His subordinates as earthly kings do, for He is perfect and without fault.

13. We have no life of our own; our life has been given to us as a gift.... As individuals, however, we have been given free will to choose. If we had no free will, we would be like animals and we would not have to answer for our actions. We must live the way God intended us to, having given us the gift of free will. We use our rational minds to discern right from wrong. We have God's judgment in us—our conscience. Every judge in the world can be bribed, but the judgment of God, our conscience, cannot be bribed. It can only be renewed through repentance.

14. When children are small they usually pray to God for their parents. Because they are young, they receive Grace. Later, when they are grown, if God wills it, they will feel joy and a state of blessedness, which is a foretaste of the Kingdom of Heaven, where angels and saints dwell. God allows this first spiritual awakening, which is received without struggle on their part, so that later their souls will yearn after the joy and blessedness they felt. When it is in this state of blessedness, the soul has no need of anything that is of this world.

Such a soul is quiet and meek and does not know anger, for the person is in a state of Grace. No one can provoke him to anger. Later this person is expected to consciously reject evil. He must defeat all the enemies of his soul while in this life. Our enemies are not made of flesh and blood, because if they were, we could hide from them or flee from them, but our spiritual enemies are everywhere. They suggest thoughts that are not rooted in love, chastity, goodness, and kindness. These noetic powers, or demons, who have different characters just as we humans do, are constantly putting impure thoughts into our heads, telling us to abandon ourselves to bodily passions, to thievery, malice, and envy. And if we listen to their suggestions and carry them out, these passions will become second nature to us.

The Holy Apostle Paul says, *The good that I would, I do not: but the evil which I would not, that I do. Now if I do that I would not, it is no more I that do it, but sin that dwelleth in me* (Rom. 7:19–20). This is the evil noetic power that has taken root in our hearts and lives in us, in our bodies. A lifetime of experience is needed to reject evil and turn toward Goodness so that nothing in this world can lead us astray from the right path.

This is why St. Isaac the Syrian says, "Preserve your inner peace at all costs and do not trade it for anything in this world." He lived in the seventh century. Because of his virtuous life he lived long.

15. We must be prepared to accept the will of God. The Lord permits all sorts of things to happen to us contrary to our will, for if we always have it our way, we will not be prepared for the Kingdom of Heaven. Neither heaven nor earth will receive those who are self-willed. God has a Divine plan for each one of us, and we must submit to His plan. We must accept life as it is given to us, without asking, "Why me?" We must know that nothing on earth or in heaven ever happens without the will of God or His permission. We must not become too engrossed with our hardships but concentrate on preserving our inner peace. Even when we are praying for something, we are trying to force our will instead of accepting God's. All hardships and sorrows that God sends us are necessary for us, but we do not understand this when we are young. When we are older, then we understand that this is the way God shows His love for us.

16. I have had many falls, sorrows, and travails throughout my life, but it could not have been otherwise. The Holy Fathers say, "How will we know that God truly loves us, if He does not take us through much suffering and sorrow?"

There are times when people become depressed and

despondent, which is a type of pride in its own way. If a person loves the things of this world, this will invariably lead to despondency, for he will not find God in them. Each human being feels lonely at times, even when he is among people, until the moment he becomes free from the things of this world. At that point, God comes to comfort him.

The soul feels lonesome because the power of Grace diminishes in it due to its interest in the things of this world. One cannot go both ways! Unless it is humbled, the soul cannot receive the fullness of God's Grace, for if it received Grace in its proud state it would surely result in great evil, as was the case with the fallen angels.

17. Our life on earth is like an *epitimia*.[1] Don't be surprised that bad things happen all the time.

18. I always long to return to the state of Grace that I had as a novice, and I cannot. My efforts are sincere; I try, but a problem arises or a thought assails me, and then I end up beset with worries. However, when the Lord sees our efforts, He does not despise us. One day He will give us the strength to free ourselves from our cares. We must leave all our cares to the Lord, leave our lives and the lives of our loved ones to the Lord, and all will be well.

19. People should be educated. Man should learn what he can. However, school only educates our minds; it does not teach us spirituality. Most of the theologians who teach in our seminaries and theological schools do not live according to what they teach. Yet they should serve as an example to our youth. They do not, and that is why the situation in our schools is not good.

School gives a person rational education, but no spirituality. However, the young should have a living example to learn from,

---

[1] *Epitimia:* a penance given to bring a soul to repentance and return it to health.

for such examples teach better than words. One can hear many edifying things on life and spirituality, but it is doubtful whether one will be able to apply this in one's life. But when one sees a person who is quiet, meek, kind, and who is never offended, then one wants to be like that person.... A living example says more than words.

A living example of a God-pleasing life solidifies theoretical knowledge and proves it in practice. This is the case not only with theology but with all other types of knowledge as well. Every kind of knowledge that we discover through education is a gift from God to His people, and it proclaims His presence in this world. The practical application of what man has been given to know is quite another matter. This depends, as I have said before, on whether we live according to God or against Him. Our knowledge is used either for the benefit of mankind or against it. All knowledge that God has given mankind is for its good; none has been given us for our destruction. It is only our free will, which is corrupt and which has lost its fear of God, that has turned the knowledge given to mankind for its own good into something evil, which is why we suffer so much in this world.

20. QUESTION: What is the most important thing in one's spiritual life?

ANSWER: To guard the peace in our hearts. Do not let this peace be disturbed at any cost. Peace should reign in our hearts—peace and silence.

Chaotic thoughts are the state of fallen spirits (demons, spirits who have fallen away from God). Our mind, however, must remain concentrated, whole, and vigilant. God can only enter a mind that is whole....

Besides guarding the peace in your hearts, practice standing before the Lord. This means being unceasingly aware that we are standing in the presence of the Lord and that He is watching us all the time. We must learn to awake with the Lord and go to sleep with Him, and eat, work, and walk with Him. The Lord is present everywhere in all things.

We can find the Kingdom of God within ourselves. "Descend into your heart, and in it you will find the ladder which leads to the Kingdom of God," says St. Isaac the Syrian.

The Holy Scriptures teach us that *the Kingdom of God is ... righteousness, and peace, and joy in the Holy Spirit* (Rom. 14:17). The first step toward communion with God is to give oneself completely over to Him. After that, it is God's energy that works in us.

Communion with God means that God has made His abode in us and that His energy is working in us. Our spirit puts on God and He governs all our feelings, our will, and our mind. We are then like a tool in His hands. He moves our thoughts, desires, and feelings and directs our words and the work of our hands.

21. Communion with God is the natural state of the soul. It is what man was created for. Man has alienated himself from this kind of life by sin, and that is why he must strive to attain it once more. All we are trying to do is to return to our former, healthy state.

When the Kingdom of God makes its abode in the heart of a person, God reveals many mysteries to him. With His help, such a person will be able to see the essence of things and understand their mysteries.

All knowledge is in God, and when He wills it, according to His mercy, He will reveal these mysteries to the mind of an individual. Even a simple, uneducated monk, by the mercy of God, can be given the gift of knowledge of the great mysteries of life and death, of paradise and hades, and learn about the inner order of things in this world.

When the Kingdom of God enters a man's heart, it is as though God takes away the veil of ignorance from his mind. Then, such a man understands not only the mystery of created matter, but also the mystery of his own being. Finally, in one sacred moment,

God will reveal Himself to him in His infinite mercy, and he will behold the King of Glory just as he beholds the reflection of the sun on the water. In such moments God and man are one, and God's Spirit works in him. Such a person lives in the world only in his body, while his spirit dwells in the Kingdom of God, with the angels and the saints, beholding the Lord.

22. God knows best what we can bear and what we cannot, and what He will or will not permit. He knows if we have the strength to fight a certain temptation. He permits a temptation to beset us in order that we might confront it with peace. Later, when the same kind of temptation comes upon us, it will go away because we will not participate in it or allow our thoughts to wallow in it.

Events happen and we take part in them. Instead of guarding our peace, we interfere with things that we should stay away from. Where the Lord permits, certain events take their course. If we have already attained peace, they will pass us by and they will not touch us. But if we take part in them, we will suffer.

23. God sometimes lets us swim into the "deep waters," and when we see that we have no more strength to keep on swimming we cry out, "O Lord, save me!" But we must paddle with our hands and at least try to keep our heads above water by ourselves. When things get critical, the Lord will save us as He did the Holy Apostle Peter.

24. We are children, and as children of the Heavenly Father we should ask for the support of our Parent. Because we were born of earthly parents, we seek support from them. But they have their cares and their worries; they are beset by all kinds of trouble and difficulties. We look to them for guidance and support, but they do not look after us. "You have a head on your shoulders—use it. You're a grown man," they tell us. The Heavenly Father, however, never avoids helping us. He is always looking after us, always

guiding us, if our heart is united with Him. But if we look for support in the world, it will be very difficult to find. It is very hard to find a person who is of one mind and thought with us.

25. The spirits of evil watch closely to see whether we pay attention to our dreams or not. They know what kind of influence dreams have on an individual and what they can do to trigger that influence. If they see that we believe in our dreams and are living in apprehension as to what we will see in our dreams, then they arrange for things from our dreams to happen, so that eventually we lose touch with reality and become incapable of living.

Bishop Porphyrius (Peric) of Jegar with Elder Thaddeus.

CHAPTER ELEVEN

ON THE FAITH

1. Some say that they are atheists, but there is no such thing as an atheist.... No such thing. Even the devil believes and trembles (cf. James 2:19), but he refuses to do good. There is no such thing as a person who does not believe in God, and there is no rational being on earth that does not long after life with all his heart. We will give anything to live eternally, and we all long after perfect love, love that never changes but lasts forever. God is life, He is love, peace, and joy. There are those who oppose Him, but they can do nothing to hurt Him. It is we who complicate our own lives with our negative thoughts.

2. No one can save us except the One Who created us. The Lord could have chosen to save us in a different manner, for He is Almighty and All-powerful. Instead, He took upon Himself our human nature and showed us by His own example the way of righteousness. Had He chosen to save us in any other way, we could say to Him, "You are the Almighty God. You were never a man as I am; You were never hungry or thirsty, sad or sorrowful." This is why God took upon Himself all of human nature. The Apostles write in the Holy Scriptures that the Lord's earthly life had many more sorrowful moments than joyous ones. No one ever saw Him laugh as we do when we are joyful; He was always sorrowful because of our sins, and He took everything upon Himself. Even today, He bears the burden of our sins. And we have not accepted Him, although He was a man just like us in all things except, of course, in sin.

3. In this life each of us has his job to do. When we, the little people, know how to go about our tasks and put things in their appropriate places, imagine how much He—Who is All-encompassing and Who provides for the whole world—knows about each thing, great or small, that is in the world. The Lord is God not only of great things but also of the small, even of those things smaller than atoms. He is God and the Creator of all. He knows how to rule over all things. Our job is to conform to Him and become of one mind with Him, for He wants His rational flock, which has wandered away from Him and His love, to return to Him. But this is very difficult for us.

4. Nothing ever happens either in the world or in the universe without the will of God or His permission. All that is good and noble is God's will, and all that is negative and bad happens because He allows it. He knows why He allows these things to happen and for how long. If the incorporeal angelic powers or we men were allowed to do as we please, there would be total chaos in the world and in the entire universe. But God is present everywhere and He is Light, a Light that penetrates all.

5. One cannot say that Christianity is a religion. Christianity is a revelation of eternity and life. The angels rejoice greatly because God has revealed Himself mystically to His creature, man. Our human nature has become part of the mystery of the Holy Trinity, and that is a great gift which we do not even appreciate; instead, we have cleaved to the things of this world. We have been given the opportunity to prepare ourselves for eternity, to vanquish evil, and to always be with our Heavenly Father.

6. Every living thing seeks love: man, animals, and plants. All people seek God and long for Him, regardless of whether they are believers or unbelievers. Some people call themselves atheists, but they do not know that in their hearts they long after God.

For when someone yearns for justice, love and truth, he is really yearning after God. All people long for love that never changes and justice that is always the same. All living things long for God. The only difference is that some oppose Him and others don't, some yearn after Him consciously while others are not aware that their yearning is really after God.

7. There will be no sleeping until the Second Coming of Christ, as some sectarians teach.[1] How can the soul sleep? The soul is always awake and active. Our bodies are unable to follow the soul in this activity and need sleep. During sleep the body and the soul are in a way separated for a time, while the body is resting and renewing its energy. During that time the soul is in a world of its own. There it can come into contact with the souls of the dead and with spiritual realms. When we wake up we very rarely remember our dreams. Of course, there are also those dreams in which the soul reproduces that which it sees and does while awake.

8. I will tell you a few words on what the laws of the Holy Church, that is, the canonical rules written by the Holy Fathers, say about those who are temporarily banned from Holy Communion. The Church does not permit those who have committed murder to approach the chalice until they have repented. Likewise, until they repent, Holy Communion is not given to those who engage in occult practices such as magic or to those who frequent so-called psychics and sorcerers. Also, women who have had abortions are under penance to abstain from Holy Communion until they have repented. This is a great sin before God, and it is a reason why such terrible misfortunes have befallen our nation. The Church also forbids Holy Communion to those who have not made peace with

[1] This false doctrine—that the soul "sleeps" or is "unconscious" after death—is taught by Jehovah's Witnesses, Seventh-Day Adventists, and others. See Fr. Seraphim Rose, *The Soul After Death,* 4th ed. (Platina, Calif.: St. Herman of Alaska Brotherhood, 2004), pp. 102n, 237–41, 249.

their friends and family, who harbor hatred for a neighbor and have not forgiven them. The Lord forbids such people to approach the holy chalice because we are all the work of His hands; we all belong to Him. If we want eternal life with Him, then we must forgive everyone from the heart.

And so, my dear ones, approach with a peaceful heart, pure feelings and a clear conscience in order to receive the most pure Body and Blood of our Lord. You see how it was the will of the Lord for us to be like Him not only in spirit, but in the flesh as well. We are His kin in the flesh, in the spirit, and in the soul.[1] He gives all of Himself to us. Do you see how He gives Himself to us without reservation? He gives us His most pure Body and His most precious Blood in order that we might have eternal life and be in communion with Him. For this He wants us to have a pure heart and to be like the angels and saints. Therefore, we must forgive everyone from the heart, for everything belongs to God. We must not have a single negative thought when we receive the Lord. If we receive the Lord while at the same time breeding hateful thoughts toward a neighbor, we are receiving Him not unto our salvation but unto judgment. And so, my children, let every one of you examine your soul and approach the holy chalice.

9. We have been baptized in Christ our Lord. We are only formal Christians; we are not as God wants us to be. There is nothing good in us—there cannot be, since we have negative thoughts and become angry, despising our neighbor. We read books, but we do not understand. Which of the philosophers and scientists has been able to say of himself, *I am the Way, the Truth, and the Life* (John 14:6)? Not one of them. Not one of them was able to say, *I am the Bread of Life* (John 6:35) or, "He who believes in Me will have eternal life" (cf. John 3:16). People are very narrow-minded. They understand very little. They are closer to lies than to the truth.

1 "Spirit" here refers to the highest faculty of the soul: the *nous* (see note on p. 58 above).

10. We are called to do good deeds, but it is not through good deeds that we are saved. If we were to be saved by our deeds, then it would not have been necessary for the Lord to come down and save us. We are saved only by the mercy of God. It is the Grace of God that saves. The Lord saves. We can get a reward for our good deeds, but salvation is from God.

11. We have not committed ourselves to the will of God—we believe that everything is in our hands and that we must decide about everything, that God has other things to do in the world. "Will He think about us?" we often ask. This means that we have very little faith and that we put very little trust in the Lord. God thinks about everything and provides for everyone. Our eyes should be on Him. For He says, *And this is life eternal, that they might know Thee the only true God, and Jesus Christ, Whom Thou hast sent* (John 17:3). This means that every event and every little detail around us and in us reveals the Lord's Divine providence and His consent. Nothing in the entire universe happens without either the will of God or His consent. Everything we see that is good and harmonious is the result of the will of God. As for anything that is in chaos, God knows why it is like that and why He has permitted it. He sets the limits. What we must know is that He is present everywhere.

CHAPTER TWELVE

ON INNER PEACE

1. We must give ourselves over to the Lord. We must commit ourselves and all that we have to Him, for He is ever present. He wants us to be quiet and at peace, with no thoughts at all. This means that the heart must keep silence. The Holy Fathers tell us that our *nous* must descend into the heart. That is where our *nous* should be, without any thoughts or imaginings. The Holy Fathers further say that we must occupy the *nous* with the Jesus Prayer. Let our minds always be saying the Jesus Prayer, for He is always present, and let us always be in communion with Him.

2. We know that the Lord, while in the flesh, was kind to all people, even those who persecuted Him—Him, the Almighty God. He showed us how to avoid evil and not oppose it. He said so Himself (cf. Matt. 5:39). Not opposing evil means preserving one's inner peace. Opposing evil is evil; it involves a desire to return evil for evil, which is what the fallen spirits thrive on. However, when they attack us and find that we do not oppose them, then our peacefulness disarms them and they are defeated. Therefore we must try to always pray like this: "Lord, help me to preserve my inner peace, teach me how to be calm and peaceful and kind, just like Thine angels."

In order to be able to do this, we must be with the Lord constantly in our thoughts. You see, we direct all our thoughts and all our attention to those whom we love. This is exactly how we should be toward God, for as our Parent, He rightfully asks that we give back to Him what He has given us. This is for our own good, in order that we may participate in Divine joy, peace, and life. Let us, therefore, learn to turn to God and seek Him ceaselessly through prayer.

3. The Holy Fathers tell us that we must preserve our inner peace at all costs and always be joyful, always in a good mood. But even St. John of Kronstadt says, "We are like the weather: now the wind is blowing, a storm is raging, there is thunder and lightning and rain—but then the sun comes out and we feel well. Then another storm comes, and so on." He goes on to say that since we are in the body, the atmospheric conditions influence us a lot. When the conditions are good, when the atmospheric pressure is not too high or too low, and when the weather is fine, we also feel well. But when the skies are gray and cloudy, we become depressed. We must learn how to preserve our spiritual balance, and when the weather is cloudy and stormy we must be at peace and be joyful.

We must try to always be in good spirits, always joyful, because the spirits of evil want us to be sad all the time.

4. You must strive to have peace in your homes. Peace starts with each one of us. When we have peace in us, we spread it around to others. You can see for yourself that there are very few humble and meek souls on the earth—but also that they are truly blessed. They will not be offended if you insult them in any way. Whatever way you treat them, they are quiet and peaceful and they are truly sorrowed because you are in such spiritual torment.

5. We are always breaking God's law. We know that the worldly authorities punish transgressions of civil law and that breaking the civil law can have even lifelong consequences. Spiritual transgressions also have consequences, even greater ones. There can be no peace in the world unless there is inner peace in each one of us.

6. As St. Seraphim of Sarov says, in order for us to have inner peace and save our souls, we must often look deep into ourselves and ask, "Where am I?" While doing so we must be careful to guard our senses, especially our eyes, so that they may be to our spiritual benefit. Gifts of Grace are given only to those who work for them by constantly guarding their souls.

7. How will we know whether we are living according to the will of God or not? If you are sad for whatever reason, this means that you have not given yourself over to God, although from the outside it may seem that you have. He who lives according to God's will has no worries. When he needs something, he simply prays for it. If he does not receive that which he asked for, he is joyful as though he had received it. A soul that has given itself over to God has no fear of anything, not even robbers, sickness, or death. Whatever happens, such a soul always cries, "It was the will of God."

8. Here on earth we are given the chance to conquer all evil with peace and stillness. We can have peace when we live in surroundings that are peaceful and quiet, but that peace is not as stable and as permanent as the peace we acquire while living in chaotic conditions. When you move from quiet surroundings to chaotic ones, your mood changes instantly and you become irritable—all of a sudden evil thoughts assail you, and your mind is in hell. That is the end of our peace. This is why the Lord guides us through sufferings and sorrows—so that we may, through them, acquire real peace. Without Him we would not have the strength to overcome these things.

There is the example of the holy martyr Catherine, who suffered for Christ when she was very young, only eighteen years old. Her tormentors threw her into a dungeon all tortured and broken, and the Lord appeared to her. When she asked Him, "Lord, where have You been all this time?" He answered, "I was here all the time, in your heart." "How can that be, O Lord, when my heart is impure, and full of evil and pride?" "Yes," said the Lord, "but you have left room in it for Me. Had I not been with you, you would not have been able to bear all these tortures. I will give you strength so that you can endure until the end."

The Holy Fathers say, "We know that God loves us when He takes us through many sufferings and misfortunes."

Peace I leave with you, My peace I give unto you: not as the world giveth, give I unto you. Let not your heart be troubled, neither let it be afraid (John 14:27), says the Lord, Who is the Way, the Truth, and the Life (cf. John 14:6).

9. You should learn to love little things. Always try to be modest and simple in everything. When the soul is mature, God will give it peace. The Lord looks upon us and is pleased when we yearn after His peace. Until such time as the soul is mature enough to receive the Lord, He will only sometimes allow it to see and sense that He is present everywhere and fills all things. These are moments of indescribable joy. But after that, the Lord hides Himself from us once again in order that we might yearn for Him and seek Him with all our heart.

10. Our spirit is saddened, everything is sorrow and suffering. You have seen for yourself: when you are in a state of peace, all is well, but here in this life, such peace does not last for long. It is disturbed very easily. For this reason we must always be in contact with the Source of life, with God—always, without ceasing. As soon as our inner peace is troubled, we must immediately ask for His help—just like a little child who, when separated from his mother, immediately cries and calls out to her. He is afraid to be alone. So it is with our soul: when it finds itself alone (separated from the Lord) it suffers a great deal, but when it is united with the Lord, no matter what misfortunes come upon it, all is well. The soul surmounts all difficulties because it is joyful to be with the Lord; it feels Divine joy and peace. The soul knows that it must

pass through the fire and water of this world in order to rise above the little things of this world that torment us. What torments us most are our thoughts. Thoughts make us do all kinds of things, then we lose our peace and are tormented by our conscience. These pangs of conscience are nothing but the judgment of God within us. And so, we must make peace with our Heavenly Father and turn to Him from our heart, asking Him to forgive us and give us of His Grace and His Divine strength in order that we may always remain in peace and joy, like the angels and the saints. Amen.

11. We have been endowed with many gifts from God, but we do not know how to live as we should, and we create hades in us and around us. Bishop Nikolai [Velimirovich] once told the story of a priest who kept asking to be transferred to another parish. After a while Bishop Nikolai answered his plea, saying, "Father, I would be glad to grant your wish for a transfer if only you were not going to take your self there!" [1]

12. When a person is in the power of the evil spirits, a false sense of peace reigns in him all the time. The devil does not tempt him with anything. We all have our periods of peace and quiet but also periods of war. The Lord permits this so that we may become well-versed in spiritual warfare and may learn how to conquer evil. Much time must pass before we attain the ability to conquer a bad trait that has been part of our personality for years, since our childhood. For this we need a spiritually experienced advisor who has himself passed through all of these phases of the spiritual life. A spiritual father or guide can teach us how to overcome such traits and how to win and preserve inner peace.

St. Isaac the Syrian says, "Preserve your inner peace at any cost. Do not trade your inner peace for anything in the world.

[1] St. Nikolai (Velimirovich) was implying that the priest would be just as unhappy in a different parish, as it was not the place but rather his inner state which was disturbing him.

Make peace with yourself, and heaven and earth will make peace with you."

13. We must always be vigilant. Vigilance and discernment are the things we need. The Lord said to Joshua, son of Nun, "Whatever you do, think it over well" (cf. Joshua 1:8).

If we at first believe that what we are about to say will be to someone's benefit, but then, after we use our discernment, we decide that our words will only hurt the other person, then it is better to remain silent. Everything should be done with discernment. When one uses one's discernment, then one is also vigilant. Vigilance is also needed in prayer. Our attention must precede our prayer. We must know what we are asking for in prayer. You see, when we ask a favor of someone, we say, "I know you can help me if you apply yourself to it." That means our attention is on the words we are saying when asking for help.

If this is the case when we are turning to a person for help, how much more should our attention be focused when we are praying to the Lord, Who is our life! But we have found ways to shorten our prayer rule: we recite our prayers by rote or read them from a book. Our hearts and our feelings have no part in such prayer, and in the end we often do not even know what we have read.

14. We can go wherever we want and do whatever we want, but that is not freedom. Freedom belongs to God. When a person is free from the tyranny of thoughts, that is freedom. When he lives in peace, that is freedom. He is always in prayer, he is always expecting help from the Lord—he listens to his conscience and does his best. We must pray with our whole being, work with our whole being, do everything with our whole being. We must also not be at war with anyone and never take any offense to heart. Let it be. Today we are offended by one person—who knows who will offend us tomorrow? We are constantly thinking about these insults, but we should just let them be in peace. We should

never take them to heart. When we do, the adversary will try to do it again, but if we just let the insult bounce off us, and remain peaceful, then people will give up trying to offend us. And people will ask you, "How come you are always at peace? Everyone else is nervous and easily offended, while you don't seem to be interested in this life at all. How did you become like that? How can you stay so calm?" Well, that is how the Lord keeps us from harm.

CHAPTER THIRTEEN

ON THE SPIRITUAL REALM

1. When I was in the Vlashki Dol parish church, a certain man came to see me and to tell me his story. Here is what he related:

He was sitting on the steps of his home, tired after a long day's work in the fields, when out of nowhere a stranger appeared. He thought that it was an unexpected guest arriving at his home, but the stranger invited him to take a walk with him. He led him away. The man had no notion where the stranger was taking him. And on they walked, when suddenly a woman appeared before them. She was full of light. As soon as she asked, "Where are you taking him?" the stranger disappeared. Then she asked the bewildered man, "Do you know where you are?" He answered that he did not. Then she struck him and repeated the question. He still did not know where he was. After she had struck him a second time, he recognized his home and the surrounding fields. She told him to go home. The man wanted to thank her, but she had vanished. Then he went home, and the first thing his wife asked him was, "What's that thing around your neck?" He looked, and it was a noose. The stranger, clearly a demon, was taking him away to make him hang himself. The man asked me to give him a little paper icon of the Most Holy Theotokos because he believed that it had been she who had saved him.

So, we can see that sometimes God permits the Most Holy Mother of God to even appear to us and deliver us.

2. A materialistic person cannot understand a spiritual person.

Anything that a spiritual person says is fantasy to a materialistic person, because heavenly logic is completely different from the logic of this world. However, when one talks to a materialistic person one may bring him to the conclusion that there is, after all, something that moves the world, and that there is harmony in the universe and disharmony on the earth.

Thus, the sons of light have been called to shine forth with their lives as much as possible and to spread the light everywhere. For the Lord Himself said, *I am come to send fire on the earth; and what will I, if it be already kindled?* (Luke 12:49). This fire is Divine love.

We Christians have been called to spread upon the earth the atmosphere of heaven, eternity, love, peace, truth, and stillness. But it is very difficult, since from our youth we have learned anger and disobedience; we have become accustomed to returning blows and to approaching everyone with distrust and reserve. We have accepted much evil into our hearts, and now we need to get rid of it.

3. St. John Chrysostom teaches us that all evil comes first from ourselves and only secondly from the devil. If we keep our minds vigilant and our hearts strong in the Faith, the devil has no access to us. The devil only acts on our own evil thoughts and wishes. When we are angry or envious, or when we have violent feelings toward someone, often or over a long period, we ourselves open the window of our heart to the demons. Then they feed our sins and nurture them, and we cannot get rid of them easily. Sometimes we wallow in a certain sin for such a long time that it becomes second nature to us. In this case only God can save us, both from our own selves and from the claws of the demons.

4. The transition from this life into eternity is a very difficult one. Before we pass on into eternity, we can pray, but afterwards we cannot do anything for ourselves—only our loved ones can help

us with their prayers. In whatever state the Lord finds us at the hour of our death, He will judge us according to it.

That is why we must pray for our loved ones who have departed this life; this is what they need from us most. The Lord hears our prayers when we pray from the heart, even though we are great sinners. The Lord is always looking into our hearts, and if we turn to Him from the heart, He will be there. He will hear our prayers even though we are very sinful, but He also expects us to repent while there is still time.

5. Once the Most Holy Theotokos appeared in a vision before one of the Venerable Fathers who wished to know how fast the movement of the spirit was. He said, "When we ask for intercession, we often receive help immediately, especially when we find ourselves in a situation that is between life and death. We receive help immediately if we cry out from the heart." The Most Holy Theotokos answered that the spirit moves at the speed of thought, and even faster. In our thoughts we can be anywhere in no time. We have not even had the time to think and help is already here. It is an unimaginable speed. Man's mind can pass through eternity in a single moment.

6. There is a constant war between good and evil. We wish to be good, but the spirits of wickedness do not want us to have a single good character trait, only bad ones. This is why we must fight. We cannot fight on our own, but the Lord is our Protector, for as soon as we ask Him sincerely to help us, He will immediately come to our aid.

Once when I was in a very difficult situation I had a vision in which the Savior told me to fall down before His Most Holy Mother, for she is the Protector and Champion Leader of monastics. This is why we must struggle constantly; this is why we have a "war of thoughts." This "war of thoughts" is not waged against flesh and blood but against the spirits of evil in high places (cf. Eph. 6:12). The Holy Apostle Paul says, *I have fought a good fight ... I have kept the faith* (II Tim. 4:7).

And so, we must always fall down before the Lord and His Most Holy Mother. We must pray to Him to make us worthy of loving Him as His Most Holy Mother, the angels, and the saints love Him. The Almighty Lord can certainly help us in this. He desires us to be like this, so that we can be with Him for all ages and throughout eternity in His love and His embrace. It is my wish that all of you pray to the Lord to make you worthy of loving Him in this manner. Then you will feel peace and stillness in your heart, for you will have given your heart to Him Who is infinite and Who can grant you boundless love and peace.

CHAPTER FOURTEEN

A HOMILY ON THE DORMITION OF THE MOTHER OF GOD[1]

I thank the Lord and the Most Holy Mother of God that He has willed to embellish this feast day of the Dormition of the Most Holy Theotokos through the angelic voices of the children who sang so beautifully. This reminds me of the days of my youth, before the war, when I was a monk in the holy Patriarchate of Pech, the Serbian Zion as some call it. The choir from Pech used to sing the responses at Holy Liturgy every feast day at the monastery. It was a mixed choir, very well organized, and the choir director was a remarkable person. I have heard many choirs from Belgrade and other places, but that choir from Pech was quite extraordinary. Today, when I said, "Blessed is the Kingdom...," the children responded with "Amen." This reminded me of those days of my youth and it touched my heart.

When the chanting is as beautiful as this, we are freed from all our cares and our interest for earthly things and we ascend into eternity with the Lord, His angels, and the saints, where our true Fatherland and our Kingdom is. If our Fatherland were of this world, then we would live here in a state of well-being, peace, and joy. However, this life for us Christians is, so to say, an *epitimia*. In this life we must prepare ourselves for life in the Heavenly Kingdom and we must attain Divine peace. No one can give us that peace; only God can give peace to created

[1] A homily by Elder Thaddeus delivered on the feast of the Dormition of the Most Holy Theotokos, August 15/28, 1984.

beings and to us if we seek Him and long for Him with all our heart and if we desire to become one with Him. He wants our souls to be united with Him, with His Divine will. He wants our entire being to become one with Him in order that we may feel the joy of living. We, on the other hand, get very involved in this material life and we have no time to think about our soul, about our inner peace. We are always shattering our inner peace.

We have many examples by which we can learn. The Lord gave us first of all the Most Holy Theotokos. It was His will that the Most Holy Theotokos remain with the holy Apostles to comfort and encourage them after His Resurrection and Ascension. One of the God-bearing Fathers, a native of Athens, St. Dionysios the Areopagite, wished to see the Most Holy Mother of God. When he arrived in Jerusalem, they took him to the home of St. John the Theologian, where the Most Holy Theotokos lived. When he entered her chamber, he was at once free of all cares and worries and was overcome with ineffable joy and peace. This is how he describes his meeting with the Most Holy Theotokos: "Had I not learned in my youth about the True God, for me the Most Holy Theotokos would have been God."

See what peace, stillness, and joy radiate from the Most Holy Theotokos! God has allowed peace and joy to radiate from every soul that is one with Him. Divine peace and joy emanate from such a person and we feel good in his presence. Do you see what the Kingdom of Heaven means? *The Kingdom of God is ... righteousness, and peace, and joy in the Holy Spirit* (Rom. 14:17).

The Most Holy Mother of God prays for us ceaselessly. She is always visiting us. Whenever we turn to her in our heart, she is there. After the Lord, she is the greatest protection for mankind. How many churches there are in the world that are dedicated to the Most Holy Mother of God! How many healing springs where people are cured of their ailments have sprung up in places where the Most Holy Theotokos appeared and blessed those springs to heal both the sick and the healthy! She is constantly by our side, and all too often we forget her.

You have seen that in this life anyone, even our closest of kin, can abandon us. We all have our weaknesses and often hurt the people closest to us. They can turn their backs on us because of our rudeness, or they can forgive us but still be hurt. But the Lord and His Most Holy Mother ... Oh, how many times have we insulted God and the Most Holy Theotokos, but when we repent and turn to them in our hearts, they forgive us everything, never remembering our sins and evil deeds!

You have already realized how unbelievably quickly life goes by. One does not notice this as much in one's youth, but when the years bear down upon us, we see that a lot of time has passed and that very little is left of this life. Where do we go when the end of our life comes? We know where we are going while we are still here, but what happens afterwards? Where are we going? Have we prepared for the Heavenly Kingdom, for our true homeland? Only the meek and those with pure hearts will enter it. Have we taken care to cleanse our heart while in this life, the heart that gives us such a hard time in this life? Have we said to ourselves, "Heart, you have caused me enough pain; humble yourself and be a patient, long-suffering heart!"

The Lord has said that we save our souls by patient long-suffering. We know that many misfortunes and sorrows come upon both the pious and the impious, both the righteous and the sinful. We all receive our share of misfortunes—this is a means of learning to accept everything in peace. On our own we have no strength, but God has strength. It is to Him that we must turn, deep down in our heart, and He will give us the strength to overcome all difficulties, for it is very important to rise above all those little things that take away our inner peace. We rarely pay any attention to this but allow the injustice that we come across everywhere in our lives to shatter our inner peace. Often we are the ones who do injustice to others. It may seem to us at the time that we are doing the right thing, but later it turns out that we were very wrong. We must learn to overcome all these little things with peace, united with the Lord, so that disquiet will not enter us from the outside, and so that we will always have our inner peace.

God is at the center of every person's life. He is in our heart whether we accept Him or not. He never separates Himself from us because He is the Giver of life Who gives life to every created being. We have buried Him with our worries and worldly cares, which destroy the peace within us, and that is why we have no peace or rest. No one on earth can give us unshakable inner peace. Money cannot give us peace, neither can fame, honor, a high-ranking position, nor even our closest friends and family. The only Giver of peace and life is the Lord. He gives peace, stillness, and joy to the angels and the saints, to us and to every created thing. Therefore we must repent and turn to the Lord.

What is repentance? Repentance is a change of one's way of life; it is discarding the old man and all of his evil habits and turning toward God, toward the Truth. Repentance means becoming quiet, peaceful, humble, and meek. Everyone knows that it is very pleasing to be in the company of a person who is meek, peaceful, and kind. A person who has no peace generates restlessness and radiates it all around, so that in the company of such a person we feel unsettled, and we too become restless. This is because we have not united with the Lord through unceasing prayer. We have peace when we are with the Lord and His Most Holy Mother; she is always here to help whenever we call upon her. In her we have unshakable support, which remains the same for all ages and which will not change. We cannot find this support anywhere else on earth, not even among our family members, let alone in things like riches, earthly power, and honor. We can be left without all these things, but the Lord and His Most Holy Mother will never leave us.

And so, my children, as we celebrate the great feast day of the Most Holy Theotokos, let us prepare ourselves for the heavenly life, let us teach our hearts to always long for God as the angels do, and for the Most Holy Theotokos, for she is our Intercessor and prays unceasingly for us weak ones before the throne of her Son. Whenever we turn to her in our hearts, she is always there to help. Countless are those on this earth whom she has comforted, and countless are the souls she has led from the depths of hades to the Kingdom of Heaven. Let us, therefore, learn to become accustomed to the Heavenly Kingdom while we are still in this life. The Heavenly Kingdom is peace and joy in the Holy Spirit. We need to humble our hearts, which take insults so deeply, and also our so-called dignity, for we cannot enter the Kingdom of Heaven in pride, as when we take to heart each slander our neighbor casts. We must accept our lessons from everyday life, for each day brings us cares, worries, and insults. We must learn not to take insults to heart, for who knows what awaits us during the course of our earthly lives? God is merciful to us and has concealed our future from us. Otherwise, not one among us would be able to go on, knowing what the future holds for him. We must live through many misfortunes and sorrows in order to learn how to rise above all these problems that disturb our inner peace. We must learn to acquire the Divine peace and joy of the angels and saints, for the Kingdom of Heaven is acquired while we are still in this life.

In this life we are in heaven one moment and in hades the next. You can see this for yourself and learn from it. When our thoughts are quiet and kind, when we forgive every slander and insult, we have Divine peace, joy, and stillness! But when we become angry because of someone's unkind words, we are at once in hades! Everything collapses, and we lose all the joy of living that we had before. Can you see how terrible living in hades is? Here, in this life, we are given the chance to taste both the heavenly life and the life of hades. We should choose that which gives us peace, the Heavenly Kingdom. We all desire this, without any exceptions, whether our lives are good or bad. All people long for peace and goodness, for ineffable love that never changes, and only God is this kind of love. He alone is unchangeable. He is always the same, and He is the basis of all things—preeminently of mankind. He is ever waiting for us to return to His embrace, but all we do is shy away from Him. He wants to give us peace and to comfort us so that we may experience the joy of living, but all we ever see are the cares and worries of this world.

From the beginning of our lives, we have all sinned gravely. The Lord has warned us to be very careful lest we have a life of hardship and sorrow, and endure much pain until we humble ourselves and realize that we have sinned. For the Lord has said, *Honor thy father and thy mother: that thy days may be long upon the land which the Lord thy God giveth thee* (Ex. 20:12). That is the law. The Lord showed us how to honor our parents by His own example when, as His suffering on the Cross was nearing an end, He entrusted His Most Holy Mother to His beloved disciple, John. He said to His Mother, *Woman, behold thy son!* (John 19:26). And to His disciple He said, *Behold thy mother!* (John 19:27).

(In the Aramaic tongue in which our Lord spoke, the word "woman" implies greater honor than the word "mother." Today, it is difficult for us to understand how the Lord could have addressed His mother as "woman." Likewise, when the Lord was in Cana of Galilee, the Most Holy Theotokos turned to Him and said, *They have no wine* [John 2:3]. And He said to Her, *Woman, what is that between Me and thee? Mine hour is not yet come* [John 2:4]. In our language, when we say "woman" this has a somewhat disrespectful meaning, but when we say "mother" it is much more intimate and affectionate. But in the Aramaic tongue, the word "woman" is much more respectful.)

See how the Lord took care of His Mother in His last hour upon the earth! What do we do with our parents? God forbid that we should continue to treat our parents the way we do. Even from our childhood we do not honor our parents, but we want to live long and well. How can we live well if we have disobeyed this God-given law from our childhood? The law of this world, which is ever changing, punishes every violation against it. How then do we expect not to be punished for disobeying the Heavenly Law?— the Word of God, which never changes, but stays the same for all ages, for it is Spirit and Life.

We are the offspring of disobedient parents. When disobedience entered our forebears Adam and Eve, our nature suddenly changed. It became corrupt, foul smelling, prone to decay, and mortal. Death entered us. Before the Fall our forebears were immortal. Only God, our Creator, can bring us back to our original state, as He created us. It is for this reason that He Who is love came down to earth and was born of the Virgin as a child. It is for this reason that He lived for thirty-three years among men. He wanted to teach us the truth and to show us that He is love. We need to look to the Lord, His Mother, the apostles and the saints as examples and renew our life. We must repent and leave behind our former way of life with all our bad habits, and we must strive to learn obedience. If anyone has hurt us—our parents, our brother or sister, a neighbor—then we must forgive them all from the heart, and when we have done so, the Lord will know. Our forgiveness must not be confined to words only. The Lord wants us to forgive from the heart. Our neighbor will then feel our forgiveness and no words will be necessary. The person will know in his heart that we have forgiven him.

How does a person know in his heart that he has been forgiven? People have thoughts. We are like a fine thought-apparatus. We are connected to each other by our thoughts. When we think of a person, he immediately receives our thoughts. But since we are distracted and our thoughts are scattered, we cannot discern who it is that is sending us thoughts or the kind of thoughts he is sending us. On the other hand, the person who has peaceful thoughts, who is united with the Lord and whom the Lord has freed from distractions, this person knows exactly which thoughts are his own, which ones come from the enemy and which ones are from friends. Feelings and thoughts coming from the minds of our fellow men reach us. This is why I say to you that when we forgive from the heart, our neighbor can feel this and the burden that has been oppressing his soul is no more.

This is the way to learn about the heavenly life and to acquire inner peace. Let us turn to the Most Holy Theotokos in our hearts and ask her to intercede for us, that the Lord might give us strength and that He might number us among His angels and saints who glorify God throughout all eternity. Amen.

CHAPTER FIFTEEN

REPENTANCE IS A CHANGE OF LIFE[1]

May the peace and joy of our Lord be upon you all! For it is true that peace and joy is the greatest wealth for a Christian both in this world and the next. We all long for it. We can have many material things, we can have everything we want, but it is all in vain if we do not have peace. And peace comes from the Fountain of Peace, from the Lord. When He spoke to His disciples while the doors were shut for fear of the Jews, the first thing He said to them was, *Peace be unto you* (John 20:19). Likewise, I too wish that the peace and joy of our Lord may come upon all of us. The Lord will reward us with His peace if we change our way of thinking and turn toward Absolute Goodness. Absolute Goodness is God Himself. He wants His children to have this Divine attribute as well. The perfection of the Christian life consists in extreme humility. Humility is a Divine attribute, too. Where humility reigns, whether it be within a family or in society as a whole, it always radiates Divine peace and joy.

Every good and bad thing on earth has its origins in our thoughts. This is why we must struggle. We are a thought-apparatus that emits thoughts, that radiates thoughts by which we influence all beings: men, animals, and plants. The plants, too, have a nervous system. They expect peace, comfort, and love from us.

[1] A sermon and talk given by Elder Thaddeus on January 31, 1998, in the hall of the "Shumadija" theater in the Belgrade suburb of Banovo Brdo. The text was first published in the *Svetigora* magazine (nos. 75–77, 1998, pp. 34–37) as recorded by Ivan Markovic.

Repentance is a change of life. One must go to a priest and confess, or tell a friend or relative if something disturbs one's consciousness and shatters one's inner peace. After confession a person always feels lighter. God has created us in such a manner that we all influence one another. When a neighbor or friend feels compassion for our suffering, we immediately feel comforted and stronger. Likewise, repentance is a change of life. We must change our way of thinking, for life has dealt us many blows. We see the entire world, not just our nation, suffering because of that. If we turn toward the Fountain of Life—God—then He will give us the strength to become rooted in good thoughts—quiet, peaceful, and kind thoughts, full of love. Our sincere repentance will shine through, for good thoughts, good wishes, and feelings of love radiate peace and give comfort to every being.

There, now you understand what repentance is all about. Repentance is a complete turning of one's heart toward Absolute Goodness, and not only of the heart but also of the mind, the feelings, the body, and one's whole being. Repentance is the unbreakable union of love with our Father and Creator. Therefore we must always be in prayer and at all times ask the Mother of God to give us the strength to love Him as she herself does, along with the saints and the angels. Then we will be blessed both in this life and in eternity as well. For God is love, peace, and joy, which fills every being that seeks Him from the heart.

And so, it is clear that if we wish good for ourselves and our neighbors, we must change. Our thoughts influence not only us but everything that surrounds us. That is why we must emit only good, quiet, and kind thoughts. The Lord commands us to love our enemies, not for their sake, but for our own good. For as long as we wallow in the remembrance of an insult we have suffered from a friend, a neighbor, or a relative, we will have neither peace nor rest. We must become free from such thoughts. This means that we must forgive from the heart. Everything must be forgiven. The peace we feel afterwards brings a sense of well-being, joy, and comfort not only to us but to all who surround us. Everyone will feel the impact of our thoughts if our thoughts are kind and peaceful. And the opposite is true, as well. If the head of a family is burdened with worries and cares about the family finances, the other members of his family have no peace. Even the little children who do not yet understand the problems of life will have no peace, because the father is burdened with cares. Therefore all of us, and especially those who have a family household under their charge, must learn to "commit ourselves and one another and all our life to Christ our God."[1] When we fully believe that God will help us if we turn to Him from our heart, He comforts us. Even if we commit a sin against our parents or disobey them in some important matter, they will open their parental hearts and forgive us and help us if we ask for their help most earnestly.

Thus we, too, must learn to forgive from the heart.

Many people come to me and tell me that they have trouble preserving their inner peace. Well, we cannot preserve our inner peace as long as our conscience is telling us something. First we must appease our conscience. The Lord will look upon us and illumine us with His Grace. And He will give us of His goodness, for goodness is a Divine power that works everywhere, especially in those who earnestly seek the Fountain of life. The Lord has said to us even through an Old Testament prophet, *My son, give me thine heart* (Prov. 23:26). This is the Divine peace that God plants like a seed in every heart and the kind of peace that gives comfort to every soul.

Our Lord is the sole comfort of both angels and men, of every soul that yearns for Him. He alone is eternal. We can seek comfort from our fellow men here in this life, but all this is very limited, for created beings are limited in time and space and cannot dispense eternity. God alone takes care of every need of our souls. Although we have been created as limited beings, we

---

[1] From the litanies of the Divine services of the Orthodox Church.

seek eternity, and no one from among our closest of kin, family or friends can give us eternity. Why? Because we are all limited beings, always at war in our thoughts. The fallen spirits are full of evil and envy, and they are constantly waging war on us. God looks upon this war in order to see whether we will seek Him and His help from the heart or not. He is always waiting to help us. However, there are few living examples in this life to whom we can look. We hear a lot of words and see a lot of examples on how to live, how to behave toward our neighbors and family, and how to instruct them to acquire peace and joy. It is doubtful whether we will apply all of this in our lives. It is quite another thing when we see a living example, a person who is quiet and peaceful, full of love—when you become annoyed, that person does not. He forgives everything and is joyful about everything. When we see such a living example, it stays with us and we yearn to acquire that kind of peace.

Life on earth is manifested in our thoughts. Whatever our thoughts are occupied with, that reflects the kind of life we lead. If our thoughts are quiet and peaceful, kind and loving, there's peace for us; and if they are negative, there's disquiet and restlessness. We are small and helpless beings, and we must unceasingly ask our Heavenly Father for help in all things; we must pray to Him to give us strength and to give us of His Grace, the Divine energy that is present and works everywhere, most especially in those souls that have chosen to serve the Lord with their whole life, both in this world and in eternity. For God is peace; God is comfort and joy to all people. I therefore wish you peace and joy in the Lord.

What more do we need—we who live in these schizophrenic times of the modern age—than peace in our hearts and in our minds, peace from the Lord? We can see and feel this peace in the humility and modesty of our white-haired holy elders, who never permit people to address them as though they were divinities or idols. That is the crucial difference between the holy elders of the past centuries and these modern newly hatched "clairvoyants."

Questions and Answers

Q. How can one stop oneself from committing a sin against one's parents who oppose the Church, who blaspheme against Christ, and who even threaten to disown us?

A. Parents have a great influence over their children. Whether they are good or bad is their own problem, and they will give an answer to God.

There is a lot of evil in the world because people have lost respect for their Heavenly Father and for their own parents. I did not know this when I was young. I take after my mother, as most men do, and like her, I am overly sensitive.

I thought that my father should do more for his children. I was his oldest son. I was born in 1914. These kinds of thoughts almost ruined my life. I should not have had such thoughts about my father. These thoughts had such a negative influence on my life—and the fact that I was a bright child did not help at all.

We must pray to the Most Holy Theotokos to give us the strength and the will to love our parents, and these difficulties in our life will disappear. The Lord will open our path and give us what is best for us. The Lord is great and He is good. He will forgive all our sins. We must love our parents regardless of what they are like. If our thoughts are good, they will have a positive influence on our parents. We must have good thoughts for the whole world. If we quarrel with our teachers or our parents, we will have hell in our souls. It has happened many times: one learns to love his teacher, and the teacher gives him good marks. If you sin against your parents, you will suffer grave consequences. Our parents have a great influence on our lives.

The Holy Fathers say, "It is impossible to have peace, yet to be full of envy and malice." Those are the properties of hades. If we can free ourselves from them, we can live a happy life. Let us pray to the Lord, for He alone can change the state of our soul.

It is better to be insulted than to insult. For if we bear an insult, we can still keep our peace; but if we insult someone, then our conscience will not give us peace.

Q. How should one prepare for Holy Communion?

A. The Holy Orthodox Church has determined the rules of preparation for Holy Communion. The main thing is to prepare the heart for uniting with the Lord. Fasting is necessary for calming the body, and once the body is at peace, the soul is at peace, too. Therefore, we are to prepare our hearts in humility and meekness for communing with the Lord. The Church teaches us how to fast. First, we must all make peace with our neighbor. Every parish priest must also make peace with his fellow men. Knowing that we are all the children of God, how can we benefit from Holy Communion if we cannot stand a certain person? If we take Holy Communion in such a state of mind it will not be unto our salvation, for we have not rid ourselves of this feeling from hades.

Fasting is the preparation of a humble heart. The Holy Fathers say, "He who has no obedience fasts and prays to God in vain. Obedience is greater than either fasting or prayer." When I was young I did not quite understand this teaching of the Holy Fathers. Later I learned why this was so. The man who does not humble himself and does not cleanse his heart from evil desires fasts in vain. He may eat nothing at all, but it will be to no avail if there is evil inside him. He must first cleanse himself from the evil within in order to receive the Lord. And the Lord is all love, peace, and joy. For this we must prepare our hearts. If we prepare our hearts to be humble and meek, full of love, then we will enjoy the health of both body and soul. If there is none of that in us, then we will be taking Holy Communion unto our judgment and not unto our salvation. That is why we always pray, "O Lord, let this Holy Communion be unto my salvation and not unto judgment or condemnation."

Q. What do you think of the popular guided tours of our monasteries and other modern trends in our church?

A. It is wrong for people to visit monasteries only out of interest for their architectural design and history. But those who go on these tours in order not only to see old frescoes but to find peace for their souls will return from their trip with joy in their souls. Even those who go to visit a monastery out of curiosity—to see the difference between monasteries built in the eleventh and in the twelfth centuries—if they have a little piety in their hearts, they will come back comforted, with a heart full of joy. On the other hand, those who visit monasteries merely for the sake of passing the time will return from their trip with an empty soul.

Q. How can we protect ourselves from those who take part in occult practices and who cast spells on us?

A. The power of magic is effective only where there is no prayer and no staunch faith in the Lord. Magic is powerless against those who pray and whose faith is strong.

Once a young woman came to see me. She had a degree in political science but was very pious in spite of all her education. She was married to a man who had previously been married to another woman. Her husband was a medical doctor. His first wife had left him after only one month of marriage. Then he married this other girl. He had an older brother who had been married three times, but all his wives had abandoned him, and he had given up trying to find a wife. Their mother was also a doctor, a professor at the medical school, and she was involved in occult practices. She was not living with her sons at the time, but with her sister. Sometimes she would visit her sons. One day she came to visit her son and his new wife, and the young woman sensed that her mother-in-law was upset for some reason. Then it came out. The older woman said to her daughter-in-law, "I sent the other one packing in less than a month, but I can't seem to get near you!" This young woman was a firm believer in the Lord, and all the magic spells that her mother-in-law was casting on her had no impact. She was, of course, trying to use the evil powers against the young woman in order that they might frighten her into leaving her husband. However, they could not get near her, for she was a woman of prayer. She had given herself over completely to the Lord, and she knew that the Lord would protect her and that the evil spirits had no power over her. What happened then was that the powers of evil turned against the older woman. She had no peace. She would come to her son and say to him, "You don't love that brat of yours, do you?" "For the love of God, Mother," her son answered, "what father does not love his son?" You see, she was trying to use her magic spells to make her son hate both his wife and his son.

Once he came home, the tears streaming down his face. "I can't bear being in our apartment. I know that this is all my mother's doing, but what can I do?" Of course, his mother had not brought him up in the Faith, he never prayed to God, and all her evil spells turned against him, while his wife was at peace. Can you see how powerful prayer is? No evil spells can touch us if our faith is strong; they only turn back on the person who is trying to harm us through these occult practices.

Q. Fr. Thaddeus, what is your opinion on cremation?

A. The burning of dead bodies is not a Christian act. It is a custom of modern times. The body of a Christian has been sanctified with the Grace of the Holy Spirit—if the person has, of course, lived a pious life—and as such may not be burned. God did not create our bodies for burning. It was His will, from the time of our forefather Adam to this very day, that when the soul leaves the body, which is dust, that dust be returned unto dust. The body should be buried in the ground and not cremated. Cremation is a modern-day invention, an attempt to save space. A person cremates his parents and keeps their ashes in an urn, believing them to be his father and mother. That is very wrong.

Q. Will the Lord forgive those women who have had multiple abortions, but have repented sincerely? What can they do to redeem their sin?

A. A woman who destroys the fruit of her womb commits a great sin. She is destroying life itself, for God alone is the Giver of life and He makes possible the conception of a human being in the womb. He gives life and a woman destroys it. Great repentance is necessary, from the depths of her soul. She must change and never commit this sin again. Otherwise, she will be condemned as a murderess. No creature on earth kills its young—only man, the rational being. This is a great sin, and if a woman does not repent from the depths of her soul, she will be condemned as a murderess. Will she pass through the toll-houses? There is no sin that cannot be forgiven but the sin of unrepentance. True and sincere repentance is required for such a sin, and it must never be repeated again.

Our people are terribly guilty of this sin. Entire villages have disappeared. When I was a child there were one hundred and ten homes in Vitovnica. Now less than half of them are still standing. It is a sad thing that we Serbs will soon be a minority in our own land, for other nations will come and populate our lands. This is very sad. People also make a great mistake when they divide their property among their children. In Germany, for example, this is not the case. Only one son stays on the farm; the others must find work. Here in Serbia, small pieces of land are divided into yet smaller pieces. What will we do when it is not possible to divide the land any further? But look at the gypsies! They have neither home nor land nor bread to eat, but their tents are full of children! It is very sad what we are doing to ourselves. Let us repent and become better, if we can!

Q. Fr. Thaddeus, what can you tell us about the souls of the dead?

A. We should not mourn the dead but instead pray fervently for our departed loved ones that God may grant them to dwell with the angels. This is what He wants from us. Mourning will get us nowhere. By mourning we not only can destroy our own health but can also harm the peace that the souls of the deceased have received from the Lord. We must pray for our loved ones. We must not be sorrowful and depressed. Excessive sorrow for our loved ones who have left this world is not a Christian act, but an act of godlessness. We prepare ourselves in this life for eternal life. We must be thankful for everything and thank God for taking the souls of our departed loved ones to Himself.

If they have departed this world without having repented, we must pray for them that God might forgive their sins. We must perform acts of mercy in their name and in their memory for the peace of their souls, and God will accept such acts of love.

Only the Lord can free a soul from the meshes of thought in which it became entangled while in this life and which still bind it in eternity. Only God can free such a soul. Therefore we must pray for our loved ones who are deceased. It is the most we can do: to pray that God grant rest to their souls and to give their baptismal names to priests and hieromonks who serve the Holy Liturgy every day so that they may pray for their souls.

Someone once approached Bishop Nikolai [Velimirovich] and asked him, "Will the souls of unrepentant sinners be saved?" He answered, "They will, if there is someone who will pray for them. It is most beneficial for departed souls if forty Liturgies are served for them and if, after that, someone gives a donation to the Church to continue commemorating them at the Holy Liturgy." The Liturgy is, as we know, a Golgothan sacrifice. This means that the Lord Himself is sacrificed at the Holy Liturgy. When a priest takes out the particles from the prosphora for the repose of the departed and after he receives Holy Communion, he says, "O Lord, by Thy most pure Blood forgive the sins of all those commemorated today!"

As you see, this is the most perfect prayer and the greatest sacrifice that we can offer up for our loved ones who have departed to God.

Elder Thaddeus.

CHAPTER SIXTEEN

COLLECTED SAYINGS
OF ELDER THADDEUS[1]

1. Our God came down among us people in order to return us to our original state, the state He had created us in. He did everything so that man could understand His will. He could have saved mankind in a different way, but fallen mankind disturbed the fine apparatus of the human mind and became incapable of good. It fell under the power of the spirits of evil, and voluntarily subjected itself to them.

2. God did not create evil. Evil comes from the noetic spirits who turned away from God's love and toward themselves and ceased to obey God, following their own way of reasoning. If a noetic power is not united to the Source of life, no matter how much it endeavors to do or say something good, all of its deeds and words are permeated with the stench of hades, for God alone is the Source of peace, joy, love, righteousness, and goodness.

3. All created beings are limited, and what is limited cannot be perfect. Created beings are given the possibility of striving toward perfection.

4. However, certain created beings are fallen beings. Certain

---

[1] The "Collected Sayings" is a document of teachings of Elder Thaddeus which were recorded during the 1990s. This document, together with a short biography of the elder, first appeared as a kind of Christian *samizdat* publication: a twelve-page self-published manuscript, typewritten and photocopied.

angels first failed to preserve their dignity and later, as a result of the envy of these fallen angels, our forebears Adam and Eve also fell. This very same trait, envy, has put down its roots in us, too. Envy stops at nothing and shouts contradictions in God's face all the time and everywhere.

5. How does envy act? Envy is a spirit from hades. It battles unceasingly against righteousness and God. God is Love, and envy cannot bear it when we do good to our neighbor. When the Lord, Who is Love, healed the old woman who had been bent over for eighteen years, evil showed its face at once and immediately began to rebel, for envy cannot bear it when good is done to anyone (cf. Luke 13:11–17). Envy never stops; the spirit of hades envies all men for all things.

6. One of the God-bearing Fathers, St. Nilus the Myrrh-gusher (he appeared to Monk Theophanes, who dwelt in St. Nilus' cave in the eighteenth century), has explained to us many of the mysteries of the Kingdom of Heaven. He said that envy was the seal of the Antichrist on the heart of man. Do you now see what a terrible thing envy is? But alas, we often envy our neighbor, even our closest of kin. We do not care even to attempt to heal ourselves from this affliction and come to our senses.

7. Jesus Christ, our God, is perfect God and perfect Man. As perfect God He encompasses all with His love, His boundless love. As perfect Man, He is dear to each soul that seeks Him. We all feel that this Divine love is somehow very far away, that God is very far away when, in fact, it is we who are moving further away from Him. He cannot move away from us, for He is life. All of Him is love. Oh, if we men could have the same love toward Him and approach Him as our only true friend! Alas, that is not how we come before Him. Instead, we are reserved, we approach Him with formality. When we pray and when we do something good,

we are altogether very formal.... He, in turn, wants us to be natural. When He came to dwell among us, He showed us the way to live: simply, humbly, and meekly. We should approach Him just as He created us—as innocent children.

8. Our Lord is pleased with the good deeds we perform. Works of mercy and everything else we do for our salvation and the benefit of our neighbor and the Holy Church, all this is pleasing to God. However, what pleases Him most is simple, innocent and childlike love which cleaves to His heart. This is what is most pleasing to Him and what He wants from us. This is what every person can give Him, rich or poor, young or old.

9. I always seem to be coming back to this subject and repeating myself: we must learn how to approach our Heavenly Father, how to come before Him with our heart and with our whole being, how to please Him as the angels and the saints do. For we are very unclean. God does not take our uncleanliness into account when we approach Him from the heart; He accepts us at once. When we sin against our Father and then approach Him from the heart, He forgives everything, as though nothing had ever happened.

10. Our Lord is boundless, and His love is ineffable. We should approach Him openheartedly and be with Him at all times, for He is with us constantly. He is the moving force of our life and wants us to understand His mind. All of His life here on earth among men was a natural life, accessible to us. He said that He was Love and explained to us that God so loved the world that He gave His Only-begotten Son for the salvation of man (cf. John 3:16). He revealed a great mystery to us, made many things known to us. He made us higher than all other creatures. Human nature, made higher than all of creation, entered into the mystery of the Holy and Life-creating Trinity.

11. What more can we, as men, wish for than to be one with our God, our Father? For this, we must learn how to approach Him in the brief time of our lives that we have been given. As we have no strength of our own whatsoever, we must approach Him as innocent, openhearted children, from the heart. We must beg Him to teach us how to be good, how to love Him as much as the Most Holy Mother of God, the angels, and the saints do.

12. The Lord will not abandon us if we always approach Him from the heart. He wants our hearts and our souls to burn with an even greater desire and longing for Him, that we may never fall away from Him and His love.

13. Often many misfortunes befall us, all because we have not humbled ourselves yet. When the soul is humble and bows down before the will of God, our suffering and misfortunes will cease. For then, misfortunes and suffering somehow become dear to us. We will come to have a completely different understanding of life. We do not reason anymore according to the laws of this world. We see everything in a different light. Everything we look upon seems somehow brighter, full of love. Everything is good because it is pleasing to God. We are His creatures and all that is created belongs to Him. He created all things for Himself, that we might be partakers of His Divine love and Divine peace and joy.

14. There, now, as you can see, we should heal ourselves. We must never allow envy to enter our hearts, for envy destroys the peace within and the tranquility of the soul. For example, we are at peace. A friend comes along and tells us about someone who has behaved unjustly toward us in the past. This person is now very successful and has achieved a lot. If we have not forgiven this person, the spirit of envy rears its head immediately. That is how it happens. We must always be vigilant in prayer, and we must never accept the suggestions of the spirit of envy.

15. The Holy Fathers say that if we reject a suggestion by the spirits of evil, we achieve victory without a battle. The Holy Fathers spoke from experience. If we reject a suggestion by evil spirits, victory is ours without a battle!

16. The spirits under heaven are always setting traps in our thoughts. When St. Anthony saw all the different kinds of nets that the spirits of evil set in order to ensnare us, he sighed and said, "O my God, who then can be saved?" And he heard a voice: "Only the meek and the humble. What is more, these snares cannot even touch them."

17. You see, when the soul is humbled, when it submits to the will of God, the spirits of evil no longer have power over it, for it is protected by the Grace of the Holy Spirit and hidden by the Divine flame.

18. Therefore, my children, let us fall down with our hearts before the Lord, let us pray to Him that He might teach us how to be good, as good as His angels and saints are. How excellent it is to dwell among the good, among those who lead a life of holiness!

19. Here on this earth people should strive to reject the suggestions of the spirits of evil. The Holy Fathers tell us always to be vigilant and to be aware that any thought that disturbs our inner peace comes directly from hades, and that we must not accept such a thought but reject it immediately. If we enter into conversation with such a thought we will soon be caught in its net. Many other thoughts will be born from that one thought from hell, and it is only much later that a person sees where his thoughts have taken him and what he has done. One evil thing leads to another, and when a person comes to his senses, he says, "Whatever made me do this? I used to be at peace, and now all of a sudden everything

has gone wrong." The reason everything went wrong is that we were not vigilant enough.

20. Love, joy, and peace are all Divine gifts, Divine properties. They can work miracles even on their own. Love unites and makes everything whole; peace radiates from a person and exudes silence; and joy takes away the pain of the soul. When a joyous person meets a sorrowful one and speaks a few kind and peaceful words, all of a sudden it is as though the sun has risen for the sad person.

Separately, love, peace, and joy work miracles, but united they can rule over all things. When they are united and deeply rooted in a person's heart, wherever that person emits a thought, there is peace, for such a person radiates peace. The Holy Fathers say that such a person can move mountains and heal sicknesses. For example, the Lord showed us how healings occur; He said that we would be able to heal sicknesses by His Divine power. These will be the signs: we will lay our hands on the sick and they will be healed (cf. Mark 16:18). Those are the true words of God.

21. However, we have lost the goodness with which the Lord endowed us, and we have allowed ourselves to be caught in the net of thoughts, like a fleeing animal, and we don't seem to be able to free ourselves. We must make sure that nothing which disturbs our inner peace enters our heart.

22. The Holy Fathers have cleared the way for us and have shown us the way to labor with the help of God. God is powerful and He can deliver us from any evil. We, however, being inexperienced, are unable to preserve that inner peace.

23. The Lord wants us to consciously, with understanding, reject evil and to accept Him and His Divine goodness into our hearts. For this, we must turn to the Lord, the only Source of life. We

must become one with Him, for we have alienated ourselves from Him. We sometimes alienate ourselves even from our closest of kin. Also, we often feel lonely even in the company of our closest family. This is because we have distanced ourselves in our thoughts from our true Father.

24. The spiritual life is the life of the *nous* and the thoughts. Therefore we must pay close attention to any thoughts we breed and pray to the Lord day and night to deliver us from all evil, to cleanse us and to give us strength to say "no" to the suggestions of the evil spirits. When we accept a suggestion, we also agree with it, and then the battle begins: we refuse one thing, then they come up with another suggestion, and then another and another ... and we are left without peace. In this case we must turn with our hearts and minds to the Lord and say, "O Lord, I have no strength, I did not learn from my youth, I have grown old doing evil and the wickedness in me has also grown old. A lot of strength is needed for me to root it out. But Thou, O Lord, art mighty and powerful; teach me to be innocent, simple, meek, and humble. Give me the gift of Thy Divine properties, with which Thou hast endowed Thine angels and saints."

25. Let us all fall down before the Lord with an innocent heart, using our own words in addition to the prayer rule that we all adhere to and which we very much need (for if we have no prayer rule, then the evil one will give us his own rule—all kinds of thoughts). That's why we need prayer, no matter how short. As soon as we are out of bed, let us give thanks to God for having allowed us to live through the night. When evening comes, let us give thanks for everything, for the Lord is the Giver of life and the Giver of all things. This is how we show our love toward Him, and because of this love, He will draw us into His embrace.

26. When the soul loves prayer from the heart it cannot bear to

be separated from its Father. It is always in His company, in His presence, either when conversing with people or while at work. Such souls are always with Him and walk in His presence, as the angels and the saints do. This is the beginning of the Kingdom of God in this life. Such souls become used to heavenly life and make the transition from this sorrowful and labor-filled life into eternal joy as ones who have already been cleansed.

27. Therefore, I wish you every good thing from the Lord and the Most Holy Theotokos, who is our great protectress. The Most Holy Mother of God is all love. I have told you before how St. Dionysios the Areopagite wished fervently to meet the Most Holy Mother of God and how he felt her presence. And suddenly he felt free from all things concerning this world and was illumined by ineffable joy and gladness. You see, this is what she wants for us at all times: for us to fall down before her from our hearts, for she is our protectress and our intercessor before the Lord. She will pray to our God, her Son, that He may give us strength to be as good as the angels and to glorify God both in this life and in eternal life.

28. No movement of thought that comes from the soul should be centered on anything that is of this world. The noetic center of our love must be God, and with God we love all. Everything is in Him and through Him. We must not become attached to things of this world.

29. The angelic hosts are not enslaved by their thoughts, or by the things of this world. They gaze upon created things, but their thoughts do not become enslaved by them, for the center of their thoughts is in servitude only to the power of God, through which they love all of creation. As for us, when we see an object that attracts us, we immediately become attached to it—this is terrible and it is also deadly. If this lasts for a length of time, then this

object becomes our idol. An object takes the place in our hearts that belongs to God, no matter whether it is an inanimate object, a living thing, or a person.

30. Divine love does not tolerate egoism. When we fall, we are empty and have no one that is close to us but our own self. We embrace the self and guard it closely, not permitting anyone to insult it, wanting everyone to think well of us. At the same time we do not notice the kind of life we live, what we do, or how we do it. We do not notice because we are so immersed in our selves.

31. We must despise the self for the sake of God's love and not only reject "his lordship" the ego, but kill him as well. For if the ego is not dead, we cannot become one with God; "his lordship" will always be in the way. Like a nobleman, the ego cannot bow its head but holds it up high at all times. This is why we need humility, we need to become humble and meek.

32. The Lord has shown us the way we should be: humble, meek, and obedient to His will. But no—we want everything to be according to our own wishes. We torture our own selves, we tire ourselves out and—what have we achieved? The world will not move the way we want it to, which makes "his lordship" very angry because things do not go according to his plan. We torture ourselves because of this, and the blame is ours. We have not humbled ourselves, we have not become one with the Lord. When we look into our hearts we see "his lordship" the ego. When temptations come along and wound us, the wound is a big one. Do you see how much healing is needed, how much humility, how much we truly need to turn to the Lord in simplicity?

33. He who has humbled himself does not think highly of himself. He knows he is nothing but dust. If it were not for the Lord preserving us and guarding us, we would be nothing but mud!

34. Have you seen Fr. Cleopas? He is very natural. It is a gift from God. He does not have a high opinion of himself. He knows that we are dust and if it were not for the Lord guarding us, we would be nothing, nothing but mud and stench!

35. The heart is always cold when the thoughts are scattered. It is only when the thoughts are gathered and centered in the heart that the heart begins to burn.

36. The heart is cold when the thoughts are scattered and when the soul is not at home but wanders about. When the soul is at home, it warms the heart. As soon as it leaves its home it receives blows. It receives blows from thoughts when it is away from home. One thought is accepted, another is rejected ... and of course, the heart is torn asunder and it grows cold, as though saying, "This does me no good and that does me no good either ..." All of this wounds one from the inside and the heart is burdened. But when the soul comes home, when it is reconciled with the Lord, then the Lord is the center of one's life and there is a feeling of goodness and warmth. We are scattered and broken, and only the Lord can make us whole again by His Grace.

37. The Lord looks at the inner depth of the heart, at what the heart longs for and what it desires. And if He sees that a soul cannot come home, the Lord will, in His own time, cleanse it and draw it to the center, and the soul will find peace. However, if in the innermost part of the heart there is something unclean, something that is attracted to this world and is bound to it, then our wandering will last a long time and we will endure much sorrow and suffering. We who are, so to speak, pious, will have more sorrow than those who are not. This is because they do not feel inner pain, they give thought not to eternity but only to things of this world: enjoyment, food, drink ... Their attention is entirely focused on this, whereas ours is divided: we want to be with the

Lord, yet we have not yet let go of material things; our heart is still attached to them and we are not free. It is for this reason that we suffer a lot.

38. The heart must break loose from its desires. If we know that all of our relationships with our fellow men and our family are but worldly things, that they bind us to the extent that our hearts become attached to them, then it is better to despise one's father and mother, one's brother, husband, and sister, because all of this is no good to us if it destroys God's peace. If this is the case, then it is better to despise all of this, become one with the Lord, and pray for His help. We must humble ourselves and then reestablish a correct relationship toward all of our fellow men. The main thing is to become one with the Lord; then He will teach us how to love our neighbor, for we do not know how—our love immediately becomes transformed into something material, for it has not been cleansed from the inside.

39. One should cleanse one's heart from worldly plans and desires. Only then can we sincerely love our neighbor. Otherwise, our earthly love will cleave first to one thing and then to another. This is a fleeting, ephemeral love and it shatters us constantly. We do not live our life with understanding but superficially.

40. In anything that we plan to do we must have one thought and one desire in mind, for this is how God wills it. He wants us all to be of one thought. The Lord prayed for us to be one. And what do we do? We are always divided, even within our family circle. This is not good. We want our own will to be done. I can understand when this happens if the head of the family is an atheist and when the Lord calls to the Faith one of the members of his family. But the person whom God has called must act wisely. He must never wage a war in his mind with the rest of the family, for then there will be no progress. In that case, the pious person becomes like an

assassin who kills his closest of kin with his thoughts and desires. It is quite another thing if we become one with the Lord, and the head of the family says, "Deny your Faith!" Then such a person cannot be our parent or our neighbor. Then we can say, "I cannot deny the Lord; I have become one with Him in my heart. I am His, and His Divine life is in me. I cannot renounce the Lord, but you, do as you will." And again, we must never think anything hurtful about this person, for even the slightest negative thought disturbs our peace. Our inner peace is disturbed, and our fellow men become hostile. Therefore, even the most fleeting thought that is not founded on love can destroy anything good.

41. In a large family it is enough for one person to be dissatisfied. The person need not show it—it is sufficient if he begins to breed thoughts of self-pity, of how he is mistreated by his neighbors— and the peace in that family is disturbed. A person can disturb the peace of the whole family with his thoughts. Then everyone is unhappy and no one knows the reason why.

42. We should have the same attitude toward all of our fellow men. We must not classify people, saying, "This one I like but so-and-so I do not." By doing so, you will have declared war on the other person and that person will not tolerate you. Even though you may not have given any outward sign of dislike by word or gesture, you have done so by your thoughts and that is enough.

43. We Christians have put on Christ at Holy Baptism. We have put on God, and God is love. How is it that, having become one with God at Holy Baptism, we wage war with Him? How do we wage war? By our thoughts! We emit negative thoughts to our fellow men.

44. As soon as we conceive a thought that is not founded on love, we have accepted the evil suggestions of the demons. By

accepting a negative thought, we accept the devil himself. The demons are invisible, but we lend them our bodies so that they become visible.

45. We see the spirit that has occupied the soul of a person in the evil that person manifests. The demon makes his appearance through that person, shouting and blaspheming. It is not the person who is shouting insults at God, for the soul is Christian, but the demon which has occupied his body, shoving him this way and that, as he pleases.

Instead of striving to understand the meaning of life, we resist it and send out wicked thoughts to our fellow men. In this manner we ourselves become evil. For as soon as such a thought is conceived in our minds, we have accepted the devil, for he is a noetic power and can enter our body. As soon as we have consented to such thoughts, he is here! How many times has he already entered and occupied the bodies of those who are pious, let alone those who are not! How many times have we shown anger toward those who have insulted us or have otherwise behaved unfairly toward us? If we think evil of such a person, it is as if we are killing him! For anything in our thoughts that unites with the feelings of the heart comes before the judgment seat of the Lord.

46. Therefore we need to recognize evil with discernment and to accept good with discernment. We must be vigilant at all times in order to prevent those with evil intentions from entering our innermost chamber. Vigilance and alertness, at all times!

47. How much greater is vigilance than even asceticism, fasting, and labor!

48. *Pray without ceasing*, says the Apostle (I Thes. 5:17). Prayer of the heart is the greatest labor one can offer to God. This is because the fallen spirits know that through prayer a man's heart

draws closest to God. The fallen spirits are always trying to make us become attached to any thing of this world.

49. When we are praying, the first thing that's needed is attentiveness. Without attentiveness prayer is not worthwhile, but if one neglects prayer completely, that is the worst. You have to work!

50. However, our attention is always wandering. The Holy Fathers have always prayed that God might deliver them from distraction during prayer.

51. We must perform every task diligently, with the Lord. The enemy is always trying to distract our mind with where we have been, what we have done, what we have heard, even from our youth. The evil spirits have a way of combining these things; they have an entire archive of all our doings.... They cannot see our inner thoughts, but they can see the state of our soul. Therefore we need a huge effort to draw our hearts close to the Lord and to be with Him at all times. This is labor-filled prayer.

52. Besides labor-filled prayer there is also Grace-filled prayer. Seeing our efforts, our desire to become one with Him, discarding all worldly desires, He releases us gradually from the cares of this world and from attachment to worldly things and brings the soul into a state of humility and simplicity. The soul no longer takes insults to heart and it becomes peaceful, accepting everything with humility. The soul gradually becomes cleansed, ready to accept the Divine flame in order to have unceasing prayer through the Holy Spirit.

53. The innocent and simple-hearted and those who are not burdened by the cares of this world are given the Divine flame of unceasing prayer sooner. On the other hand, we who are curious to

COLLECTED SAYINGS OF ELDER THADDEUS

know this and that are overburdened with the cares and interests of this world—we need time to be renewed, to abandon our worldly cares, to be reborn.... However, we cannot do this on our own; the Holy Spirit needs to come down and enter our heart and push out all the worldly things so that the wisdom of this world no longer occupies it. Then we will be one with God. It is only then that the Lord grants us true wisdom and true, deep knowledge about all existing things. The heavenly mysteries are revealed in proportion to the degree of a person's humility. To a meek and humble person is given to know the mystery of everything that surrounds us. Such a person has a spiritual understanding of all things. He has a more profound understanding than those who have spent years studying the wisdom of the world. The key to the mystery is in God, and until they can free themselves from the wisdom of the world, men cannot have complete knowledge of things. They may think that they have achieved much, that their knowledge on a certain subject is great, but as long as they see things in that perspective, Divine wisdom cannot enter their minds and hearts. To such people only superficial facts are given for their efforts in studying medicine or physics.

54. In the spiritual realm thoughts are as clear as speech; they can be heard. For this reason the labor one invests for the betterment of one's soul is more valuable than any other gift. If we do not prepare ourselves for eternity by correcting our characters, we will not be able to enter the company of the angels and saints. Then we will pass into eternity with all these faults and sins.

55. As long as we have even the slightest support from anything that is of this world, we put very little trust in God. The Holy Fathers always accepted both fortune and misfortune as coming from God, and they achieved humility. When He sees that a soul is ready, the Lord sends the Grace of the Holy Spirit upon that person, and he receives the gift of freedom, peace, joy, and

consolation. There is no more fear. As for us, we are always full of fears.

56. Until a person is illumined by the Holy Spirit, fear is always present. Afterwards there is no fear. Such a soul has compassion for everyone; he understands that all creation suffers because of the Fall of man. Such a person is always ready to weep for all and to pray for all.

57. In this world it is possible for a person to expend great effort and labor for the good of his fellow men, yet for his soul to remain soiled with sin. A person can pass through most of the toll-houses, yet be pushed into the abyss as he reaches the toll-house of mercy, for in spite of all his efforts he failed to notice that his heart was firmly bound to the powers of hades. He may have performed many good deeds in his lifetime, many souls may have been saved through his efforts (say he built many churches), but if he did not focus on cleansing his soul, then the attachment of his thoughts to the things of this world will not permit him to enter the world of eternal values that can be perceived by clean souls only. Such a person is under the rule of the spirits of wickedness, according to the level of his unmercifulness. Even during his earthly life he is in their power. When his soul departs his body, such a person will be in their power.

58. We cannot be saved without fighting against the devil! We are the descendants of our parents, from whom we have inherited all those negative traits that are not easy to get rid of. We must suffer heartache in order for our souls to be freed from these mental bonds. Our enemy attacks either directly or else indirectly, through other people. And so we fight—according to the Lord's providence—and we gradually come to our senses. Without misfortune there is no prayer to God.

59. And so we come to realize that our support here in this life is nil. "There is no one who can understand me," we say. The soul seeks unchangeable love, but there is no such thing here on earth. Only the Lord can comfort us.

60. To the degree that we let go of our worldly cares, the Lord allows us to feel that He is with us. The Lord is peace, joy; He is father, mother, and friend to us. We have everything in Him. He is the One Who satisfies the needs of the soul.

61. When a soul becomes one with the Lord, it must always keep vigil. We are still in our bodies, through which we are attached to the things of this world.

62. Often the Lord allows the enemy to surprise us, and we wonder: what has happened to us? The Lord permits these things to happen in order that we might realize we are nothing and the trust we place in ourselves is nothing. We must learn to never ascribe any merit to ourselves.

63. We must always be careful to please the Lord in every deed or thought. Yes, even in our thoughts. Every task we perform in this world is God's work.

64. If we loved the Lord with all of our heart we would never fall into sin as long as we lived, for He would be with us. He is the power by Whose flame every unclean thing and every sin is burned. Nothing unholy would ever enter our hearts.

65. Because we live in the flesh and are unclean, whenever we wish to show our love for our neighbor, our bodily passions interfere. We must separate love from the passions. The passions are the fruit of the demons. We must focus our attention on Divine love,

which does not discriminate. Divine love is not egotistical; it is all-encompassing and finds joy in all things.

66. The warfare of thoughts and the enslavement by thoughts ... this is an unceasing battle. It never stops. However if a person, with God's help, becomes more knowledgeable in blocking the attacks that come in the form of thoughts, he will know that these attacks are from the devil and will cry out, "O Lord, what filth is in me! Along came the thought that so-and-so insulted me, and this thought will not abandon me.... After that, I heard about the war in such-and-such a country and the injustice that is being carried out there. And again my thoughts will not leave me in peace, and I begin stating my opinion. All of a sudden my peace is shattered—I have begun to pass judgment...." We must leave everything to the Lord. He will take care of everything in the world. Our thoughts should not become involved in these worldly matters. If we let them do that, we will always be at war with the world, fighting with words and thoughts, and we will not have peace. At the end of our earthly life it will turn out that we have become accustomed to constant arguments!

67. A tempest of thoughts and confusion of the mind after a person has confessed and heard the advice of his spiritual father means that the person has succumbed to pride and that he is waging a war in his thoughts against his spiritual father. The Lord sees this and permits temptations to befall such a person.

68. When a person loses Grace, he does not realize it for quite some time, thinking that he is still in a state of Grace, for his thoughts are still alive. He does not realize that he has grown cold and is in peril of losing life eternal.

69. Put a humble and meek person into hades, and he will not complain.

70. Great temptations (suffering) come before or after the good that the Lord gives us. This happens so that the soul may not be filled with pride.

71. The Lord desired to become incarnate from eternity, for He knew that rational beings would not preserve their state. We must return to our original state, of being pure, meek, humble, and good, in order that we may be in communion with God, Who is love.

72. It is only when man enters into communion with the angels and saints that the soul is able to understand the Divine. The Lord sometimes allows this to happen to an ordinary person. When a suffering person has no comfort, no consolation from anyone on earth, when he feels despised and rejected by everyone, then the Lord Himself comforts this soul.

73. All those fallen noetic powers are circling the earth. Every sin is a property of the fallen spirits. Every sin is [first] a thought, a powerful thought.

74. The fallen spirits try to find "consolation." Some of them look for it in wrath and anger, others in desperation, yet others in fornication. Even among the fallen spirits there are different degrees of wickedness.

75. One must always be natural and devoid of all conceit. As soon as one becomes conceited, it is quite clear where the conceitedness comes from—from the fallen spirits that circle around.

76. While it is in the body, the soul is protected, but when it is out of the body, it is completely unprotected, naked and vulnerable, like a snail when it is taken out of its shell.

77. If a soul remains in humility, then the Lord enlightens it more and more.

78. There are people who are united with God to such an extent that no unclean thoughts ever touch their minds. They never enter into any kind of contact in their thoughts with the fallen spirits.

79. We see from the example of St. James the Faster that the goal of the fallen spirits is to force men to commit sins so that they may lose the gift of healing and miracle-working. However, one must also know this: there have also been those who fell into sin although they led a holy life. This was because they had not cleansed themselves completely of all impurity. There is the example of a certain virgin who fell into the sin of pride to the extent that she came to despise all married people.

80. Philosophical purity lasts for as long as a person's thoughts are immersed in philosophy. We must attain a purity that is a result of our love for God.

81. We are very distracted and our concentration is weak. We are like a broken mirror that reflects reality in small fragments until the power of God makes us whole again, able to faithfully reflect His image.

82. If the Lord were to answer all our prayers according to our faith, what would happen is that we would think we no longer needed advice from anyone, not even from the Church. Also, the devil could interfere with someone's health, and we might be asked to pray for the sick person. Then the devil could withdraw from the sick person—ostensibly by our prayers—and we would fall prey to spiritual delusion.

83. When we demand respect and attention from others, they

usually turn their backs on us; but when we give no thought to the respect of others and care nothing about it, then people flock around us and follow us.

84. Our wicked thoughts generate evil and disturb the peace in the universe.

85. What is the velocity of movement of the angels? Angels are spiritual beings and the velocity of the spirit is equal to the velocity of thought. The velocity of thought is the velocity of the spirit.

86. If the soul is not revealed through the body, it is exposed through thought. At night the soul communicates with the noetic world. The demons always prey upon a pious soul that is full of light. They want to suffocate such a soul; it is as though a rebel has appeared in their dark realm. We permit the spirits of evil to approach us through our pride.

87. During sleep and upon awaking the soul can be in different states. When the soul is at peace, the thoughts are rested. In another instance, a person goes to bed rested, but in the morning arises all broken and tired, as though he had been laboring at some cumbersome task all night, and his thoughts are restless. It is as though a film strip were inside his head showing him scenes from the past and at the same time blurry plans for the future appear. From these "intrusions" the soul makes its own combinations. When the soul is clean from these combinations and from stress, then the person's dreams are peaceful, and he awakes in the morning rested and renewed. It is possible for us to even wage war with the souls of other people in our sleep and to argue with them.

88. Literature is often the result of the lies of the fallen spirits. Such novels and books are not Christian works; there is even Satanism

and lies in some of them, for Satan is the father of lies. If a person fantasizes, he is immediately caught in the net cast by the evil spirits. The devil then tells him, "See, you are like me now!"

89. The Lord permits many disappointments, sorrows, and misfortunes to befall us in this earthly life in order that we might stop placing our trust in the world, which harms us so much, and that we might realize that He alone is the Source of all comfort, peace, and stillness.

90. When the devil cannot harm us by turbulent thoughts, he attacks us through peaceful thoughts. It is only after we have spent some time building something founded on these pseudo-peaceful thoughts that we come to realize clearly who is really behind them.

91. A person comes to a monastery who does not fully understand why he is there. So he starts leading a worldly life in the monastery. Such a person cannot bear to see someone growing in the Faith, and he departs from this world with this character trait which he has been unable to correct. If this is our situation, then we must always pray to the Lord like this: "O Lord, help me to correct this flaw of my character!"

92. The Lord will not answer every prayer, for if we were to receive fulfillment of our prayers whenever we ask for something, we would be convinced that no one on this earth is wiser or more deserving than we are. We would believe that we do not need anyone's advice on anything. Sometimes the Lord reveals to us answers to certain questions and mysteries in our thoughts, but sometimes He does not, so that we might turn to other people for advice and so humble ourselves.

93. We are usually angered when someone insults us or ridicules

us, until Divine Grace comes upon us. When we receive Grace, we no longer feel hurt when others insult us but remain quiet and peaceful, as though the insult was not directed at us at all.

94. When there is an argument, we always go out of our way to convince the other person that he is wrong. That is how the atmosphere becomes tense. The other person argues and will not accept our correction, and as for us, we are wasting our time and disturbing our inner peace for nothing. If we have discernment, we will know who it is who is really talking. We will know that it is not our "opponent" but the fallen spirit speaking through him. It is useless arguing with those who have been waging war against mankind for thousands of years and who are very agile and practiced in this warfare against people.

95. What is fasting? Fasting is not so much abstinence from food as abstinence from impure thoughts.

96. When an evil spirit sees that a person is trying to please God and is making progress in the good, it finds its way into the hearts of other people and from there it envies the godly person. In this manner the fallen spirit creates an evil disposition in other people toward their brother, and they feel envy toward him. Under the influence of the demon they commit many evil and malicious deeds against their brother, spread lies and rumors about him, and disturb him as he goes about his business. To us it seems as though men are the ones who envy their pious brother, but it is really the spirit of wickedness that has secured its place inside the heart of those people and is envious. Likewise, the spirit of evil enters the heart of a person who has heard that misfortune has befallen a man with whom he has not had a good relationship for a long time. He doesn't know that it is the spirit of hades that is rejoicing at his neighbor's misfortune.

97. A spirit can occupy a space much larger than the volume of the human body, but it can also occupy a much smaller space, even as small as one cubic centimeter. Therefore it is possible that an entire legion of fallen spirits may enter a person. They rejoice when they occupy a person's body, when they become "incarnate" in a human body.

98. Therefore, may you be granted every good thing by the Lord, and also by His Most Holy Mother, who is our Protectress and Intercessor before God. She will ask her Son, our God, to give us the strength to be good and to glorify God, both here on earth and in eternity. Amen.

ACKNOWLEDGMENTS

The material that comprises *Our Thoughts Determine Our Lives* was translated from the Serbian book *Peace and Joy in the Holy Spirit* (*Mir i radost u Duhu Svetom*) (Belgrade: "Obraz," 2004). The latter book was the first attempt to present all that was available of Elder Thaddeus' life and teachings. Mainly transcribed from recordings of the elder, the book consists of talks, conversations, and sermons in their original length.

To minimize redundancy, we have organized Fr. Thaddeus' teachings by subject. At the end of the book we have included a sermon and a talk in their entirety to give a more complete view of how the elder presented his teachings. We would especially like to thank Barbara Toonder for her initial editing of the translation.

The material for the Life of Elder Thaddeus included in this volume was taken primarily from the Introduction to *Peace and Joy in the Holy Spirit* written by Matej Arsenijevic. Other information included in the Life was gathered from the elder's own words in his conversations and talks, and from recollections of his spiritual children.

We would like to thank all those who diligently labored to publish the original book in Serbian: Priest Srdjan Jablanovich, who received a personal blessing from Fr. Thaddeus to publish a book such as this one (on the condition that it be made public after his repose), and who lent many audio-cassettes and texts; Priest Dragoslav Topolac, who graciously lent several photographs of the elder, audio-cassettes, and a photocopy of his "Collected Sayings of Elder Thaddeus"; Vladimir Stefanovich, who gave numerous audio-cassettes and CDs with the recorded voice of Elder Thaddeus; Mira Brishevich, who diligently, word for word, transcribed the elder's teachings and sermons; Milinko Stefanovich, through whom the publishers discovered some important photographs of the elder; and Jovan Srbulj, editor for the "Obraz" publishing center at the St. Alexander Nevsky Missionary School, who made possible the publication of *Peace and Joy in the Holy Spirit.*

INDEX

Page numbers for illustrations are in boldface italics.

SAINT HERMAN
OF ALASKA
BROTHERHOOD

Since 1965, the St. Herman of Alaska Brotherhood has been
publishing Orthodox Christian books and magazines.

View our catalog, featuring over fifty titles, and order online, at

www.sainthermanpress.com

You can also write us for a free printout of our catalog:

St. Herman of Alaska Brotherhood
P. O. Box 70
Platina, CA 96076 USA

OUR THOUGHTS DETERMINE OUR LIVES

Typeset in Adobe Garamond.
Printed on sixty pound Glatfelter Offset paper
at Thomson-Shore, Inc., Dexter, Michigan.